D0868256

The
Listening Side
of
Prayer

The
Listening Side
of
Prayer

Dr. J. C. Hash, Sr.

Insight Publishing Group

The Listening Side of Prayer by Dr. J. C. Hash, Sr.
Published by Insight Publishing Group
8810 S. Yale
Suite 410
Tulsa, OK 74137

This book or parts thereof may not be reproduced in any form, stored in a retrieval system or transmitted in any form by any means—electronic, mechanical, photocopy, recording or otherwise—without prior written permission of the publisher, except as provided by United States of America copyright law.

Unless otherwise noted, all Scripture quotations are from the King James Version of the Bible.

Copyright © 2000 by Dr. J. C. Hash, Sr.
All rights reserved
ISBN: 1-930027-18-4
Library of Congress Catalog Number: 00-104496

Printed in the United States of America

Dedication

To my best friend and lifelong companion, Joyce—without your faithful love and prayers through the years, our wonderful marriage or this book would not exist.

To my children, J. C., Jr. and Melinda, Arthur and Cherie, Brian and Virginia, Jayson and Mia, and all of my grandchildren—may your lives be filled with an abundance of the same love and joy you have given to me and your mother/grandmother.

To my parents, the late Bishop R. K. Hash and Mother Mildred Hash—for your love and faithfulness to me and to each other through the years. I appreciate the heritage you have worked so hard to provide and protect for me, Joy, your children and your grandchildren.

Contents

A Personal Word
by Oral Roberts

While reading this remarkable manuscript by my friend and fellow co-laborer in the gospel, immediately it caused me to remember the importance of the listening part of my personal prayer life.

Having ministered in the great church of Bishop James Hash, Sr., having been in his home and served with him as a fellow Trustee of the International Charismatic Bible Ministries, I have been given an inside view of his prayer life. When I share with him or hear him preach, I'm aware that he has "heard" from God as well as "talked" to God in prayer. I feel it in my spirit.

In a positive way, I see James as a mentor to better help each of us both to pray vocally and then spend as much time listening to God rather than talking back to Him.

Our God is a talking God; we are a listening people, and listening is equally important. Thank God for this book. I treasure it.

—Oral Roberts
Oral Roberts Ministries
Tulsa, Oklahoma

Introduction

I know for a fact that every believer who is alive in the earth today has prayed at least once—at least to be born again. Even if a person just uttered the words, "Oh, God, save me," he prayed. Simply speaking to God is one of the ways we can pray.

However, even though I know every believer who is alive today has prayed, many have not received the full blessing God intends through prayer. God intends prayer to be the connection between Himself and His people. It is the lifeline of communication and interaction. It is the essential link in our fellowship with Him.

God has called us into a loving relationship. In any relationship there must be communication to bring about life and happiness in that relationship. Likewise, we must communicate with God to have a fellowship full of life and joy.

In the best relationships there is effective two-way communication. We must see the importance of what that kind of relationship with God entails. Furthermore, we must learn to tap into the very depths of the heart of God in order to have a meaningful relationship with Him. The most effective means of cultivating a meaningful relationship with God is through prayer.

That is why prayer is vital to our success as believers. Not the kind of prayer where we do all of the talking. Prayer is a dialogue, not a monologue. To pray effectively, we must listen to God as well as speak. Listening is the side of prayer that holds the answers to all of our problems, our decisions and our dreams. Unfortunately, it is the side of prayer we often forget, or perhaps have never learned to master. I call it "The Listening Side of Prayer."

The listening side of prayer occurs when you learn how to listen to and hear the voice of God. When you learn this, then you can truly walk the Spirit-filled and Spirit-led life. You can truly be empowered to succeed at every juncture in life. Simply put, every time you need to know what to do, or which direction to go, you will not only know how to ask God for help, but you will be able to listen and hear the answer! It is a fail-proof way to live.

As you read this book and study the truth I'll be presenting to you, ask the Holy Spirit to make it come alive on the inside of you. Ask Him to teach you the "listening side of prayer."

Chapter One

What Is the Listening Side of Prayer?

A fter we pray, there should be a listening part of our prayer session. It is the time when we listen to God rather than talk to Him. The listening side of prayer is a "learned" skill. It is not merely a matter of being silent so that God can speak. Rather, it is an acquired skill that involves our attitude, our ears and our time. It also involves knowing the various ways in which God speaks and includes the ministry of the Holy Spirit. Like all skills, this skill must be developed by learning to listen to God with our spiritual ears.

When we listen, we are willing to listen to God's voice through whatever means He chooses and thus obey what He tells us to do. Obedience is the key to blessings. In prayer, it is not so much what we are saying to God, but what He is saying to us.

> If any man have ears to hear, let him hear. And He said unto them, Take heed what ye hear: with what measure ye mete, it shall be measured to you: and unto you that hear shall

more be given. For he that hath, to him shall be given: and he that hath not, from him shall be taken even that which he hath.

—MARK 4:23–25

Most Christians want to develop the "faith walk": how to speak in tongues, how to shout, how to praise and so on. These things are all great and very necessary to having a powerful Christian walk, but they will amount to very little if we do not train our ears to listen to God. Nothing in the life of a Christian is more important than listening to the voice of God. We can try to accomplish many things in life, but if they're not what God is telling us to do, then we defeat ourselves and waste our time.

Listening to God's voice can bring you out of any situation—it will guide, direct and make provision for you even in your most dry season. God knows every situation before it happens and He will always warn you of things to come. The devil doesn't ambush you because God is very much aware of the devil's plots. As Christians, we get into trouble when we do not take time to hear from God. We end up making decisions based upon our flesh instead of the Spirit of God. Furthermore, these decisions often lead to serious trouble. God desires to deliver you from that situation, but if you do not learn to hear and heed His voice, there is little that He can or will do for you.

Listening to God is the key to reaping your blessings. But you will only reap according to the way you hear.

Our ability to hear from God and our obedience to what we hear are what make us different from the world. As praying believers, our prayers are not complete until we take the time to listen to God after we pray. Otherwise, we will only have what is called "one-sided prayer," which is ineffective.

> He that is of God heareth God's words: ye
> therefore hear them not, because ye are not of
> God.
>
> —JOHN 8:47

Unfortunately, most Christians are guilty of doing all
the talking during prayer. They never allow God time to
do any talking or responding to them. Listening to God is
the key lesson we all need to learn in order to turn our personal lives, families, marriages and businesses around.

What does God have to say about the situation? What is
He trying to say to you about the matter? What does He
have to say about you and what you are doing? What does
He have to say about what you want to do? After it is all
said and done, the most important opinion is not ours,
our spouse's or our best friend's. It is God's opinion and
direction that we need.

THE SUCCESS CONNECTION:
WHY LISTENING IS SO IMPORTANT

There are many Christians that have not learned how to
tap into the listening side of prayer. Many have gone to
Bible School and consider themselves successful, but they
are not really experiencing the success that God has for
them. They have become successful in their own ability.
Always remember, true success that is everlasting comes
from hearing the voice of God and obeying it. In fact, the
word *success* is only mentioned once in the King James
version of the Bible.

> This book of the law shall not depart out of
> thy mouth; but thou shalt meditate therein day
> and night, that thou mayest observe to do

according to all that is written therein: for then thou shalt make thy way prosperous, and then thou shalt have good success.

—Joshua 1:8

It is interesting that most people spend their lives trying to be successful. Many view obtaining wealth, children, a profitable business, nice homes and other material possessions as achieving success and spend endless hours in pursuit of these things. These people are forever looking for a secret formula to bring about success and fail to realize that success is a part of God's plan. In all of their studying, searching and sweating, they fail to turn to the ultimate source for the formulas and secrets He has for their success.

And it shall come to pass, if thou shalt hearken diligently unto the voice of the Lord thy God, to observe and to do all his commandments which I command thee this day, that the Lord thy God will set thee on high above all nations of the earth: And all these blessings shall come on thee, and overtake thee, if thou shalt hearken unto the voice of the Lord thy God. Blessed shalt thou be in the city, and blessed shalt thou be in the field. Blessed shall be the fruit of thy body, and the fruit of thy ground, and the fruit of thy cattle, the increase of thy kine, and the flocks of thy sheep. Blessed shall be thy basket and thy store. Blessed shalt thou be when thou comest in, and blessed shalt thou be when thou goest out. The Lord shall cause thine enemies that rise up against thee to be smitten before thy face: they shall come out against thee one way, and flee before thee seven ways. The LORD shall command the blessing upon thee in thy storehouses, and in all that thou settest thine hand unto; and he shall bless thee in the land which the LORD thy God giveth thee. The LORD shall establish thee an holy people unto himself, as he hath sworn unto thee, if thou shalt keep the commandments of the LORD thy God, and walk in his ways. And all people of the earth shall see that thou art called by the name of the LORD; and they shall be afraid of thee. And the LORD shall make thee plenteous in goods, in the fruit of thy body, and in the fruit of thy cattle, and in the fruit of thy ground, in the land which the LORD sware unto thy fathers to give thee. The LORD shall open unto thee his good treasure, the heaven to give the rain unto thy land in his season, and to bless all the work of thine hand: and thou shalt lend unto many nations, and thou shalt not borrow. And the LORD shall make thee the head, and not the tail; and thou shalt be above only, and thou shalt not be beneath; if that thou hearken unto the commandments of the LORD thy God, which I command thee this day, to observe and to do them: And thou shalt not go aside from any of the words which I command thee this day, to the right hand, or to the left, to go after other gods to serve them.

—DEUTERONOMY 28:1–14

You can see that everything a person could hope for is promised in these verses. To position ourselves for these blessings all we have to do is to "hearken to the voice of the Lord our God." According to Webster's dictionary, the word *hearken* means "to hear with attention or interest; to obey diligently; to give heed to; to yield to; or to listen to."

God gave success to people in the Bible when they sought Him and hearkened to His voice. In 2 Chronicles 20, King Jehoshaphat sought God when he was about to be invaded by several enemies. He set his face to seek God and prayed the prayer of petition for the people of Judah. Amazingly, God answered him and destroyed his enemies without Jehoshaphat ever having to lift up his sword! Because he trusted in the Lord, hearkened unto his voice and taught the people to do the same, the Lord made them abundantly wealthy and prosperous with the spoils of their enemies.

Furthermore, the people of the Bible that were successful and prosperous learned to stay in God's presence and to hearken unto His voice. The same is true today. Most of the major ministries around the world will tell you that their success is not their own, it is God speaking to and moving through them. They stay in the presence of God. They never make a move without *first* consulting Him.

For example, Dr. Paul Yonggi Cho, founder of Church Growth International of Korea, pastors the largest church in the world. When once asked what he attributes his church growth and success to, his response was . . . "I pray and obey."

Kenneth Hagin, Sr. ("Dad Hagin" as he is known by many) of Rhema Bible Training Center once said that on many occasions God has spoken to him so audibly that he turned around. It was as if someone was standing behind him! Now, I believe that there are levels of walking with God. I also believe that God brought Dad Hagin to such a high level that he actually felt the presence of God behind him as He spoke to him.

Wouldn't that be an awesome thing to experience on a regular basis? Hearing God's voice so often and with such familiarity that whenever He spoke to you, you actually felt His presence! But Dad Hagin did not get there overnight, and neither will you. You must take the first step and start where you are. The longer you seek Him, the better the relationship and communication get. It is just like being married. The longer you and your spouse are together, the more you are able to understand one another. In the beginning stages of marriage, you probably had problems understanding one another. The same principle is true when walking with God. In the beginning stages you may have problems understanding, but you can not give up. You must press in, keep working, keep walking and keep listening. Eventually, just as in a marriage, you come to the place where you can really communicate. That is when true joy comes. Until you are able to effectively communicate, there will be a lot of confusion.

Until you learn how to hear from God, nothing good that happens in your life will last. Degrees, education and natural training are all good, but they can not compare to the divine wisdom of God that comes from hearing, seeing and living by the Spirit. Remember Psalm 127:1 "Except the LORD build the house, they labour in vain that build it: . . ." God should be the builder of everything in your life. He said that He would teach you how to prosper or profit, and that He would show you the way that you should go. (See Isaiah 48:17.) What better guarantee of success can anyone ask for? There are a number of things that men can do, but if God is not in it, it is nothing but vain work.

This is something that we must all learn because we all

have talents and abilities. Quite often, because of our talents and abilities, we find ourselves operating in the strength of a man instead of listening to and seeking the divine wisdom and direction of God. We try to do things in our own ability and our own timing.

Now do not misunderstand what I am saying. We should work and put forth our faith. But, before we do, we need to see what the Word says and listen to God's still, small voice to get His direction.

In Matthew 7:24 Jesus said: "Therefore everyone who hears these words of mine and puts them into practice is like a wise man who built his house on the rock" (NIV).

The "rock" that is referred to in this passage of scripture is the revealed knowledge of God's Word. Jesus also said in Matthew 7:26,

> . . .every one that heareth these sayings of
> mine, and doeth them not, shall be likened unto
> a foolish man, which built his house upon the
> sand . . .

A good way to know whether or not you are hearing the voice of God is by examining your obedience to the instructions God gave you. If you are really hearing, you will obey. If not, the instructions are falling upon deaf ears. To put it plainly, you really are not hearing. As stated in the passage above, only a fool will hear and not obey. There are many Christians that hear and do not obey. This indicates one of two things: either they are foolish or ignorant. I will leave it to you to determine which you are: a fool that hears and does not obey or a wise man that hears, obeys and is therefore blessed.

Chapter Two

You Can Hear From God

If you are a born-again believer, you have the ability to hear from God. Jesus Himself often spoke in parables so that only those who were believers could hear and understand what He was saying.

And the disciples came, and said unto him, Why speakest thou unto them in parables? He answered and said unto them, Because it is given unto you to know the mysteries of the kingdom of heaven, but to them it is not given. For whosoever hath, to him shall be given, and he shall have more abundance: but whosoever hath not, from him shall be taken away even that he hath. Therefore speak I to them in parables: because they seeing see not; and hearing they hear not, neither do they understand. And in them is fulfilled the prophecy of Esaias, which saith, By hearing ye shall hear, and shall not understand; and seeing ye shall see, and shall not perceive: For this people's heart is

waxed gross, and their ears are dull of hearing, and their eyes they have closed; lest at any time they should see with their eyes, and hear with their ears, and should understand with their heart, and should be converted, and I should heal them. But blessed are your eyes, for they see: and your ears, for they hear. For verily I say unto you, That many prophets and righteous men have desired to see those things which ye see, and have not seen them; and to hear those things which ye hear, and have not heard them.
—MATTHEW 13:10–17

Throughout the introduction and first chapter, we continually made the point that prayer is a two-way communication with God. However, before we get into the meat of the listening side of prayer, let us stop and examine who qualifies for this. The answer is that only the born-again believer has a communication link to God. That may come as a surprise or shock to many who have been "praying" for years, but let us see what the Bible says.

But know that the LORD hath set apart him that is godly for himself: the LORD will hear when I call unto him.
—PSALM 4:3

In this passage, David says that those who are set apart, sanctified, people of God (saints) are the people God hears.

Now we know that God heareth not sinners: but if any man be a worshipper of God, and doeth his will, him he heareth.
—JOHN 9:31

Here again, we see qualifications placed upon the ability to communicate with God. If God hears only us, it is not effective prayer. The Bible also gives us many passages concerning our ability to hear from God. In fact, Jesus, Himself, often spoke in parables, knowing that only certain people, those who believed, would be able to hear and understand. (see Mark 4:23–25) We see the following verse repeated over and over throughout the scriptures:

> He that hath an ear, let him hear what the Spirit saith unto the churches.
> —REVELATION 3:22

The Amplified Bible says in that same scripture:

> He who is able to hear, let him listen to and heed what the [Holy] Spirit says to the assemblies [churches].

Since we see that He speaks to those who are able to hear, then there must be those who are not able to hear. In order to find out who those people are, we need only to go to the Master Teacher and find out what He says about the matter.

> If any man have ears to hear, let him hear. And he said unto them, Take heed what ye hear: with what measure ye mete, it shall be measured to you: and unto you that hear shall more be given. For he that hath, to him shall be given: and he that hath not, from him shall be taken even that which he hath.
> —MARK 4:23–25

Notice that in this passage, Jesus reminds us that the

person who has received will have more given to him. We
have been given the gift of being born again. With that
awesome gift comes many other gifts by the Spirit. Our
Father has set apart many things for us that the unbeliever
cannot have; but the gift of understanding and hearing
Him and His Word is one of the greatest of these.

Now realize this: people of the world *hear*, but they do
not *listen*. Their ears are not in tune with the voice of the
Spirit. They have no perception of the truth in the Word
because they do not have the power of the Holy Spirit.
They cannot begin to comprehend the true meaning of
what the Word says and the promise God has for His
people.

> But we speak the wisdom of God in a mystery,
> even the hidden wisdom, which God ordained
> before the world unto our glory: Which none of
> the princes of this world knew: for had they
> known it, they would not have crucified the Lord
> of glory. But as it is written, Eye hath not seen,
> nor ear heard, neither have entered into the heart
> of man, the things which God hath prepared for
> them that love him. But God hath revealed them
> unto us by his Spirit: for the Spirit searcheth all
> things, yea, the deep things of God. For what
> man knoweth the things of a man, save the spirit
> of man which is in him? even so the things of God
> knoweth no man, but the Spirit of God. Now we
> have received, not the spirit of the world, but the
> spirit which is of God; that we might know the
> things that are freely given to us of God. Which
> things also we speak, not in the words which
> man's wisdom teacheth, but which the Holy
> Ghost teacheth; comparing spiritual things with

spiritual. But the natural man receiveth not the things of the Spirit of God: for they are foolishness unto him: neither can he know them, because they are spiritually discerned.

—1 CORINTHIANS 2:7–14

So we see here that as born-again believers, we have another ear—the ear of the Spirit. We no longer have to listen with our natural ear. We were changed in the new birth so we are able to hear with our spiritual ears.

Unbelievers, however, have not been changed to hear from the Spirit. Because they are not submitted to God, they cannot hear God's voice.

Verily, verily, I say unto you, He that entereth not by the door into the sheepfold, but climbeth up some other way, the same is a thief and a robber. But he that entereth in by the door is the shepherd of the sheep. To him the porter openeth; and the sheep hear his voice: and he calleth his own sheep by name, and leadeth them out. And when he putteth forth his own sheep, he goeth before them, and the sheep follow him: for they know his voice. And a stranger will they not follow, but will flee from him: for they know not the voice of strangers.

—JOHN 10:1–5

All that ever came before me are thieves and robbers: but the sheep did not hear them.

—JOHN 10:8

And other sheep I have, which are not of this fold: them also I must bring, and they shall hear

my voice; and there shall be one fold, and one
shepherd.

—JOHN 10:16

But ye believe not, because ye are not of my
sheep, as I said unto you. My sheep hear my
voice, and I know them, and they follow me:

—JOHN 10:26–27

Here we see that Jesus is the way, and we, who are His
sheep, know His voice and follow Him. So, as the fol-
lowers of God, we have the advantage of hearing from
God, which those who are unbelievers cannot do because
they do not have the power of the Holy Spirit to discern
what God says to the church (the called-out ones, the set
apart ones, the saints, the believers, the born again.)

So, as this chapter closes, if you are a believer, rejoice
that you are uniquely qualified to hear from God. Thank
God for giving you this ability that saints have as a part of
our inheritance.

Giving thanks unto the Father, which hath
made us meet to be partakers of the inheritance
of the saints in light:

—COLOSSIANS 1:12

However, if you are not a believer, but you would like to
hear from God and be lead by His Spirit, it all starts with
salvation. Pray this prayer now:

*Dear Lord, I believe that You are the God of
Abraham, Isaac and Jacob, the God and Father
of the Lord Jesus Christ. I come humbly before
You, acknowledging that I am a sinner and*

asking that You forgive me of my sins. I come to You in the merit, holiness and righteousness of Your Son. I believe that He is Your Son. That He was born of the virgin Mary, died on the cross at Calvary for my sins and was buried. And that on the third day, You raised Him from the dead and that He ascended into heaven and is now seated at Your right hand. I accept Your Son, Jesus, as my Lord and Savior. I am unified with Him in all life and work, including His promised Holy Spirit—fill my spirit, and my mind with Your Spirit. I give my body to the Holy Spirit's control and transformation. I submit all my being to the Lordship of Christ.

My spirit rejoices in fellowship with the Father, the Son and the Holy Spirit. I offer up this prayer to You, my heavenly Father, in the Name of the Lord Jesus Christ by the power of the Holy Spirit with thanksgiving.

As one who is now qualified to hear from God, this does not mean you can hear correctly. Being a believer is just like having a degree from college; it only gets you in the door.

Let's look at the requirements that will enable us to clearly and correctly hear from God and follow Him in every situation.

Chapter Three

Hearing From God: The Requirements

What is the condition of your heart? Your heart has everything to do with how you hear from God. He speaks to His people by sowing His Word into our hearts.

A RIGHT HEART

Look at the parable of the sower. Jesus gave examples of the different types of people that hear the Word according to the state of their hearts.

> And He said unto them, Know ye not this parable? and how then will ye know all parables? The sower soweth the word. And these are they by the way side, where the word is sown; but when they have heard, Satan cometh immediately, and taketh away the Word that was sown in their hearts.
>
> —MARK 4:13–15

These are people who are not really guarding their

hearts as the Word instructs us to do. They hear the Word by occasionally coming to church, hitting and missing; or they come to church and really do not pay attention to the Word being sown into their hearts. They hear it but do not heed to it.

> And these are they likewise which are sown on stony ground; who, when they have heard the Word, immediately receive it with gladness; And have no root in themselves, and so endure but for a time: afterward, when affliction or persecution ariseth for the Word's sake, immediately they are offended.
>
> —vv. 16–17

These are the people who have hard hearts. They hear the Word and are offended by it; especially when the Word is a word of correction. Their hearts are full of weeds that are choking the Word because they are not attending to the seed properly. They feel that the Word being ministered is aimed at them maliciously, and they do not want to obey it. They hear it and receive it, but when Satan comes to test it, they let it go. The Word did not take root. Therefore, when persecution comes for the Word's sake, they take offense and Satan steals it from them.

> And these are they which are sown among thorns; such as hear the Word, And the cares of this world, and the deceitfulness of riches, and the lusts of other things entering in, choke the Word, and it becometh unfruitful.
>
> —vv. 18–19

These are people that hear the Word and are often bitter

because they are too troubled by the cares of the world and things not going as they feel they should. They have their eyes on the hand of God instead of the heart of God. Their desire for things, riches and lusts is so important that it has become like thorns in a garden. Now do not get me wrong; I believe in the prosperity message. I believe that God wants His people blessed, rich and to have the desires of their hearts. But He wants to have your heart and know that you have His. Then He will bless you so that the things He gives you will not have you, but you will have them.

> And these are they which are sown on good
> ground; such as hear the word, and receive it,
> and bring forth fruit, some thirtyfold, some
> sixty, and some an hundred.
>
> —v. 20

These are people who guard their hearts. They have a heart after God just as David did. When they make a mistake, they are quick to repent and they do not harbor evil thoughts in their hearts. These people love the Lord with all of their hearts and do all that they can to keep their hearts pure by striving to walk in love at all costs. They believe the Word, receive the Word and obey the Word. Therefore the Word bears fruit in their lives.

Notice what Jesus says to those with a pure heart in Mark 4:21–24:

> And he said unto them, Is a candle brought to
> be put under a bushel, or under a bed? and not
> to be set on a candlestick? For there is nothing
> hid, which shall not be manifested; neither was
> any thing kept secret, but that it should come
> abroad. If any man have ears to hear, let him

hear. And he said unto them, Take heed what ye hear: with what measure ye mete, it shall be measured to you: and unto you that hear shall more be given.

If you develop your spiritual ears and take heed to what you hear, there will be nothing hidden from you in the Word of God. The more you hear and receive the message in the Word and obey it, the more He will reveal His Word to you that you may hear even more. Now I would say that's a pretty good reason to want to develop your spiritual ear. We will discuss how you can develop your ears in a later chapter.

If you would like the Lord to heal your ears so that you can begin to hear from Him, put your hands on your ears and pray with me:

> *Father, I desire to hear from You. I ask in the Name of Jesus Christ, my personal Lord and Savior, that You develop my ears to hear. Help me develop a listening ear of the Spirit that I may be conscious of Your voice and Your work. Help me to be patient to wait upon You and not to move until I know beyond a shadow of a doubt that I have heard from You. Anoint my ears to hear Your voice, Father. Teach me, Holy Spirit, to understand the voice of God, to listen to God, and to be patient enough to hear God in this day and hour. Father, I know that the most important thing in my life is to hear from You: to develop a hearing ear and to obey You. I must develop a hearing ear. Teach me to hear, Holy Spirit. Through You, I will take time to hear from God, my Father.*

Beloved, I want you to know that if you believe the prayer that you just prayed, you have taken one of the most important steps in being able to hear from God.

THE HOLY SPIRIT

In John 16:13 we are taught that the Holy Spirit will not even speak until He has heard from the Father . . .

> Howbeit when He, the Spirit of truth, is come, He will guide you into all truth: for He shall not speak of Himself; but whatsoever He shall hear, that shall He speak: and He will shew you things to come.

If hearing from God is that important to the Holy Spirit, it surely makes it pretty important for you and me. That which you do not see and hear is what the devil can or will try to use to destroy you. To say the least, the Holy Spirit is a good teacher. Not only is He a good Teacher, He is *the Teacher*. He speaks and moves only as the Father tells Him, and I think we should follow His example. He is the Miracle Worker and the One who makes good things happen in the earth.

God wants us to develop our spiritual ears to hear from Him. In prayer, learning is of primary importance. That is why the Holy Spirit wants to teach us how to use our ears twice as much as we use our mouths. The ears lead the way to the tongue. However, in most cases, people who are dull of hearing use the tongue to lead the way to the ears. They are often quick to speak and slow to hear. But the Bible says to be quick to hear and slow to speak (James 1:19). When we speak before we know what is going to happen, we get into trouble.

> Howbeit when He, the Spirit of truth, is come, He will guide you into all truth: for He shall not speak of Himself; but whatsoever He shall HEAR, that shall he speak: and He will shew you things to come.
> —JOHN 16:13, EMPHASIS ADDED

The Holy Spirit will not speak until He hears, and neither should we.

If we are going to walk in the wisdom of God then, like the Holy Spirit, we must learn not to speak until we hear what God says. We need to practice learning how to be silent. It would serve us well to follow after the slogan What Would Jesus Do? The only way we'll know what Jesus would do or say is to be quiet and listen to the Spirit long enough to find out! This would prove beneficial to us no matter what we face or what decisions we need to make.

You must settle in your heart that you will not move until you know what the Lord would have you to do. There may be times when you have to make a quick decision, but if you do not have to make a quick decision, then don't! Spend some time before God. Until you have that peace in your heart, do not move. In the natural you may want to do one thing, but God may be telling you to do something else. What He tells you to do may even seem foolish to the natural man. But remember, God often uses the foolish things to confound the wise (1 Cor. 1:27).

God wants us to be blessed. He wants to help us make decisions. However, we often limit the power of God because we are too impatient to listen to the Holy Spirit.

THE TONGUE OF THE LEARNED

> The Lord GOD hath given me the tongue of
> the learned, that I should know how to speak a
> word in season to him that is weary: he wak-
> eneth morning by morning, he wakeneth mine
> ear to hear as the learned.
>
> —ISAIAH 50:4

The scripture above says that God will awaken our ears to hear so that we might speak. This is one of the main scriptures that the Lord used to deal with me over and over again when I began to teach on the subject of the hearing ear many years ago. In this one scripture there are two very important things we need to learn about hearing from God.

First, "The Lord has given us the tongue of the learned." The tongue of the learned is the tongue of the Spirit. If anyone should have the answer to the problems of the day, it should be Christians. We should have a word for that person that is weary, worried and does not know what to do. We are to set the pace for the world because we should spend time with God and hear from Him. Everywhere we go, people should run to us because we are the men and women of God that say nothing until we have heard from God. They should know that we do not say the first thing that comes into our head. We will say what the Word says and what the Spirit of God instructs us to say. That is the tongue of the learned: the tongue that says only what God says.

Second, "He awakens us every morning to hear as the learned." How does God awaken us? By our ears. We cannot speak with the tongue of the learned until we first hear. We can speak without hearing, but it will not be with the tongue of the learned. It will be us and our big mouths. God would prefer to awaken us by speaking into our ears; then we can speak a word in due season to that person who is worried. It all goes back to what Jesus taught His disciples in the parable about the Sower. Paraphrasing Luke 8:18, ". . . and to him that has heard, more shall be given. But he that has not, that which he seems to have shall be taken away." As God awakens our ears to hear it makes us different from the world. It is what takes us over and makes us the head and not the tail. It is what blesses us and keeps us out of the curse. It is what causes us to be rich and not poor. It is what causes us to be strong and not weak. It is what causes us to represent God in every situation.

Let's look at Isaiah 50:4 in the New International Version of the Bible.

> The Sovereign LORD has given me an instructed tongue, to know the word that sustains the weary. He wakens me morning by morning, wakens my ear to listen like one being taught.

The "tongue of the learned" is shown as the instructed tongue, to know the Word that sustains the weary. This simply means that God wants to give us the Word we are to speak as we all go our different ways in the course of the day. He wants to use us, the salt of the earth, to speak the Word that will sustain those who are "going through," troubled or in need of encouragement. If we go into the earth with the right tongue, then we are the preservers of the earth. He tells us in Joel 3:14 that there are multitudes waiting in the valley of decision. God has given us a fresh word for them by awakening us morning by morning to hear the Word He has to say. Again, you cannot be taught until you have ears to hear, for He awakens our ears and not our tongues.

Look at what David says in Psalm 4:4.

> Stand in awe, and sin not: commune with your own heart upon your bed, and be still.

As you meditate on this verse, you will begin to see the importance of getting quiet before God so that you can hear what God has to say. The greatest advice in the world is the advice of the Lord. Evermore, He is willing to give His advice for every area of your life, your business, your family, your work, your children and everything that concerns you. God wants you to prosper in every area of your life, but you will not until you practice hearing from Him.

We must hear from God! As we begin to develop the ear of the Spirit, God will begin to awaken us early in the morning to give us a fresh word for the day.

Now God will awaken you, but if you are not conscious of the leading of the Spirit you will not know what to do. Would you like a tip? Just be quiet. That's it—plain and simple. *Be quiet!* All you need to do is to practice listening. This is one of the major areas that the body of Christ needs to grasp: practicing silence and listening to God. Praise God for the Holy Spirit, for He is the Teacher who will teach us to be quiet and hear from God. He will also give us the tongue of the learned. He is the Teacher, Instructor, the Guide, Revealer of the Truth, and the One that brings things (the Word of God) to our remembrance that produce peace.

One reason why so many of us do not have learned tongues is because we give God so little chance. We try to command Him to heal our loved ones, move our mountains and do everything that He has empowered us to do. But how often do we take the time to hear what *GOD* is saying about our loved ones, our mountains and the things we are talking to Him about? God may want you to give your loved ones a word and start teaching them. They may have some unforgiveness in their lives, and God may want you to go to them and help them see it. You do not know what may be going on in their lives. There could be problems with strife or something else. But instead, we cry out to God "heal, heal, heal" and we do not know what is causing their illness in the first place.

The one thing I do know is that God knows.

It could be something in their personal life, their professional life or even their business. There could be one *minor* thing that the devil is using against them that you do not know about. But God knows it, sees it and will reveal it to you if you just take the time to listen. Likewise, in your own situation He will start to deal with you in a particular area that will capture your spirit. You will not be able to get away from it because God constantly leads you in that direction. But do you know what? God will not do anything until He can get you to hear. As much as He desires to bless you, He will not do anything until you hear and obey what He is saying. You must obey, for the blessings are in obedience. Do not limit God — learn to hear and obey what you have heard.

Don't jump out there and try to do something in your flesh. There are many things that look appealing and exciting to your flesh or may even look like the answer to your problems. But what is God saying about your life? What is God saying that you should do? What God says is the most important thing. God already has a plan for your life, but you will not walk in it until you hear from Him. Don't get so busy that you act before you hear.

HAVING AN EAR TO HEAR: THE SPIRITUAL EAR

Most of us know that there is a natural man and a spiritual man and that there are celestial beings and earthly beings. If we have to develop our natural members intellectually and physically, then it stands to reason we also need to develop our spiritual members in the same way.

Look at Matthew 13 again. Although we dealt with part of this scripture earlier, I need to reiterate a few things before we move forward.

> Who hath ears to hear, let him hear. And the disciples came, and said unto him, Why speakest thou unto them in parables? He answered and said unto them, Because it is given unto you to know the mysteries of the kingdom of heaven, but to them it is not given. For whosoever hath, to him shall be given, and he shall have more abundance: but whosoever hath not, from him shall be taken away even that he hath.
>
> —MATTHEW 13:9–12

Remember, this chapter deals with the *spiritual* ears and eyes. When asked why He spoke in parables, Jesus explained that the parables are only intended to be interpreted by those that have spiritual ears to hear or understand what is being said. The parables are mysteries of the Kingdom and only intended for the born-again believer. They are not intended to be understood by the unbeliever or the natural-minded, unregenerated man. Unbelievers cannot understand the things of God; they are foolishness unto them because they are spiritually discerned (1 Cor. 2:14). Jesus was saying that whosoever hears with their spiritual ears and understands what is being said in the parables will receive greater spiritual understanding. And those who cannot hear with their spiritual ears will eventually lose what they already have obtained.

Let me give you an example of what Jesus was saying. God, as our Father, wants to give His children wisdom, knowledge and advice just as a natural father would his natural children. He does so through His Word in parables and by the voice of His Spirit in our spiritual ears. The Bible teaches us in Matthew 7:11 that:

> If ye then, being evil, know how to give good gifts unto your children, how much more shall your Father which is in heaven give good things to them that ask him?

God wants to bless us. He wants to provide for us. He wants us to hear His still small voice so that He can lead, guide and direct us. Isn't this what any natural father would want to do for his children? Again, if a natural man, being evil, would want to do good things for his children, how much more would your Father God want to do good things for His children?

As an earthly father, if I saw my son playing outside and a snake approached him, don't you think I would do all that I could to save him? I would be a sorry father if I did not yell and warn him. I would warn my son to get into the house or run for cover because I could see what was coming. Because I love him so much, I would not dare let the enemy come in and do him harm. Well, since God sits high and looks low, He will warn us of sudden danger if we have an ear to hear. Without that ear, what do you think would happen?

Now in the example I gave of my son, if he was deaf he

would not be able to heed my warning. This is the case with so many Christians today. God warns us because He sees everything that the devil is trying to do. He sees every attack and every attempt the devil makes against us. Unfortunately, when He warns us, most of the time we do not have an ear to hear.

God is always speaking, but we just have not developed our spiritual ears to hear Him. Therefore, the enemy comes in and steals from us; he tries to destroy us and take from us that which God intended for us to have. But Jesus said, "he that has an ear to hear let him hear." (Matthew 13:9) Do you have an ear to hear? There are a number of individuals that never take the time to develop their spiritual man, especially their spiritual ears.

Let's return to Matthew 13 and begin with verse 13,

> Therefore speak I to them in parables: because they seeing see not; and hearing they hear not, neither do they understand.

In this one scripture Jesus deals with the spiritual eye which sees by the Spirit; the ears, which hear by the Spirit; and the heart, which understands by the Spirit.

> And in them is fulfilled the prophecy of Esaias, which saith, By hearing ye shall hear, and shall not understand; and seeing ye shall see, and shall not perceive: For this people's heart is waxed gross . . . (v. 14)

This is where you find most Christians. Their hearts are heavy to the things of God. They are hard to the things of God and give no place to the Word. " . . . and their ears are dull of hearing . . ." They do not like the Word of God.

They like everything but the Word. Singing and praise is wonderful, but when it is time for the Word they sit on the pew and go to sleep. Their minds are on everything from dinner to television, but they give no place to the Word. Furthermore, when that happens, they develop dull ears and heavy hearts. They have no love for the Word, which, when it is all said and done, is the only thing that will help them to survive. " . . . and their eyes they have closed; lest at any time they should see with their eyes, and hear with their ears, and should understand with their heart, and should be converted, and I should heal them."

The Bible says, "out of the mouth of two or three let every word be established." (See Deuteronomy 19:15; Matthew 18:16 and 2 Corinthians 13:1). Let's establish what the Word says about the spiritual ear.

By the Spirit of God, Paul spoke about the spiritual ear in Acts 28:26–27.

> Saying, Go unto this people, and say, Hearing ye shall hear, and shall not understand; and seeing ye shall see, and not perceive: For the heart of this people is waxed gross, and their ears are dull of hearing, and their eyes have they closed; lest they should see with their eyes, and hear with their ears, and understand with their heart, and should be converted, and I should heal them.

Now Paul did not have the Book of Matthew. When he spoke this, he spoke it under the unction of the Holy Spirit quoting Isaiah 6:9. And yet he confirmed what I have said: there is a spiritual ear and a natural ear; there is a spiritual eye and a natural eye; there is a spiritual heart and a natural heart. Unless you develop your spiritual members, especially your spiritual ear, you will miss out on or fail to comprehend many of the things of God. Beloved, we must develop the listening side of prayer.

He goes on in Acts 28:28 to say,

> Be it known therefore unto you, that the salvation of God is sent unto the Gentiles, and that they will hear it.

Put your fingers in your ears and pray this with me. "I will hear with a spiritual ear. God, remove the wax out of my ears. Remove the dullness out of my ears and take the heaviness of my heart. The deafness of my ears must be removed. I rebuke it and I command it to leave in Jesus' Name. Lord, give me a hunger for Your Word."

A third witness is found in Mark 4:23–25.

> If any man have ears to hear, let him hear. And he said unto them, Take heed what ye hear . . .

Watch what you hear. Watch what you allow your ears to hear. Do not let your ears be a garbage disposal to everyone's gossip.

> . . . with what measure ye mete [or hear], it shall be measured to you: and unto you that hear shall more be given. For he that hath, to him shall be given: and he that hath not, from him shall be taken even that which he hath.

The measure of what you hear from God will determine the measure of what you will reap.

Now do you see the importance of learning how to hear from God?

> For nothing is secret, that shall not be made
> manifest; neither any thing hid, that shall not be
> known and come abroad. Take heed therefore
> how ye hear: for whosoever hath, to him shall
> be given; and whosoever hath not, from him
> shall be taken even that which he seemeth to
> have.
>
> —LUKE 8:17–18

God wants us to know everything. He hides things in the Word for us, His children. When the Word of God goes forth, its purpose is to enlighten us. If we are of Him then we will hear His words (John 8:47). Therefore, we must take the time to develop our spiritual ears. Once we develop our spiritual ears, God can tell us how to get our other spiritual members in order. But again, we must take heed to how we hear. If we are not hearing from God, little by little, the devil will steal the Word from us and all that God intends for us to have.

I want to give you a couple of other scriptures. Look at Proverbs 2:1–6,

> My son, if thou wilt receive my words, and
> hide my commandments with thee; So that thou
> incline thine ear unto wisdom, and apply thine
> heart to understanding; Yea, if thou criest after
> knowledge, and liftest up thy voice for under-
> standing; If thou seekest her as silver, and
> searchest for her as for hid treasures; Then shalt
> thou understand the fear of the LORD, and find
> the knowledge of God. For the LORD giveth
> wisdom: out of his mouth cometh knowledge
> and understanding.

Developing our spiritual ear is a part of receiving the wisdom and knowledge of God. We have to want it, seek it, cry out and search for it. If we knew that there was a large piece of gold or buried treasure under our house, we would do all that we could to get it, would we not? God wants us to know that our greatest riches are in the wisdom, knowledge and understanding—all of which come out of His mouth. He alone knows where we can find riches, treasures and blessings. But we must tune our ears to hear Him. We must search in His Word and seek Him for understanding of that Word. It is there; it is ours. God wants us to have it. But we have to want it and have an earnest desire in our hearts for the things of God.

Search for it as you would search for gold, knowing it is there and searching for it until you find it.

Notice what the Word says in Proverbs 8:1–11,

> Doth not wisdom CRY? and understanding put forth her VOICE? She standeth in the top of high places, by the way in the places of the paths. She CRIETH at the gates, at the entry of the city, at the coming in at the doors. Unto you, O men, I CALL; and my VOICE is to the sons of man. O ye simple, understand wisdom: and, ye fools, be ye of an understanding heart. HEAR; for I will SPEAK of excellent things; and the OPENING OF MY LIPS shall be right things. For my MOUTH SHALL SPEAK truth; and wickedness is an abomination to my lips. All the WORDS OF MY MOUTH are in righteous-ness; there is nothing froward or perverse in them. They are all plain to him that under-standeth, and right to them that find knowledge. RECEIVE MY INSTRUCTION,

and not silver; and knowledge rather than choice gold. For wisdom is better than rubies; and all the things that may be desired are not to be compared to it.

—PROVERBS 8:1–11, EMPHASIS ADDED

Talk about a mouthful! There are some great nuggets in this passage of scripture. I have taken the liberty of emphasizing the words in this passage that particularly relate to God speaking to us and our hearing Him. One cannot get wisdom, which is more precious than rubies, silver and gold, without *hearing the words of wisdom and receiving them.* Instead of placing all of our confidence in natural things, we need to place our confidence and value on the things of God—hearing and understanding His divine wisdom, knowledge and truth. There is NOTHING that can be compared to the wisdom of God. Nothing can take its place! While the rest of the world chases after the gold and the silver, we need to chase after the wisdom of God, for therein lies all the silver and gold or anything else we need!

Wisdom is truth, and Jesus said that " . . . the Spirit of truth, is come, He will guide you into all truth: for He shall not speak of Himself; but whatsoever He shall hear, that shall He speak: and He will shew you things to come. He shall glorify Me: for he shall receive of mine, and shall shew it unto you" (John 16:13–14). If the Holy Spirit speaks what He hears from Jesus (truth) and then speaks these things to us and shows them to us in order to glorify Jesus, it seems to me that we ought to put ourselves in position to *hear* what He has to say.

Are we any better than Jesus and the Holy Spirit? We learned earlier that Jesus only spoke what He heard from the Father (John 8:28; 12:49). And now we have learned that the Holy Spirit only speaks what He hears from Jesus. Now if hearing the voice and words of Jesus is good enough for the Holy Spirit, it certainly is enough for me.

All we need in life is to hear from Jesus. He is more than enough, and He is all that we need. If I have one word from Jesus, what can man do to me? What can the devil do to me? We have it all in Jesus! Glory to God! We can make it in life without man or woman, person or earthly things, but we cannot make it without Jesus. We need to seek for Him like we would silver and gold and refuse to be satisfied until we have Him. We cannot afford to let anything or anyone take His place.

Once you have learned to hear from God and understand His wisdom, God has a promise for you which is found in Proverbs 8:12.

> I wisdom dwell with prudence, and find out knowledge of witty inventions.

One idea from God can bring abundance into your life. It can bring all the gold, all the precious jewels, all the pearls and everything we think we need apart from Him. I'm sure you have heard it said time and time again "One word from God can change your life." His words and thoughts are what bring favor and prosperity. That is one of the reasons we need to develop our spiritual ear to hear the voice of God and know His thoughts.

We can put all of our attention on wealth and prosperity while giving little attention to spending time listening to God. Now do not get me wrong. I strongly believe and teach it is God's will for us to prosper. (See 3 John 2.)

But any man or woman who wants prosperity without wanting the wisdom and instruction of God is a fool! (Proverbs 1:7, 32; 15:5).

In Proverbs 8:13 we are told that "The fear of the LORD is to hate evil: pride, and arrogancy, and the evil way, and the froward mouth, do I hate."

Without hearing from and reverencing Him we can get into pride and arrogance, which is the evil way. We fall into believing Satan's lie that *we*, not God, had everything to do with our prosperity and favor. We start to think that we somehow deserve some type of credit for what God has done for us. But always remember, Proverbs 16:18, "Pride goeth before destruction, and an haughty spirit before a fall." Therefore, beware the spirit of pride. We must keep a humble and contrite spirit.

Chapter Four

Developing the Listening Side of Prayer

We are about to enter into the nuts and bolts of the listening side of prayer. Before we continue, if you are serious about developing this awesome part of your spiritual life, pray this prayer aloud. I have prayed this prayer over my congregation, and we have seen God manifest Himself in some very wonderful ways.

> *"Father, thank You for revealing Yourself to me. Thank You for revealing to me Your plans and Your ways for my life. Thank You for giving me direction and guidance that I may have the tongue of the learned and the ear of the Spirit. Father, I pray that the things which I have read will have an impact upon my life. I pray that I will develop the tongue of the learned, the ear of the Spirit and the eye of the Spirit. May I continually please You in everything that I do. And I will forever give You the praise, the honor and the glory for the good that is done in my life. For I know that every good thing that hap-*

pens is because of You and Your Son Jesus. It is not because of me, but because of You. Fill my cup and let it overflow with your blessings. In the name of the Lord Jesus Christ I pray, praise, honor and thank You. Let it be known, Lord, that my heart's desire is to be like You and to help others to do the same. I desire more of You in my life Lord, more of Your life and Your Spirit. Change my character, my words and my ways. It is all about You, Jesus. It is all about You.

If you have prayed this prayer with sincerity, you are now to begin to develop the listening side of prayer.

Preparation

Step One: Developing the Tongue of the Learned

There are several steps in developing the tongue of the learned. First and foremost, you must learn how to understand the Word of God. Your inner ear must be sensitive to the Word of God. (See John 8:47.)

When you go to pray, always take a piece of paper to write down what the Spirit tells you.

Second, knowing the Word will help you to know God. The Bible is the greatest book that anyone will ever know. Its whole purpose is to help you to know the Lord God.

We read and study the Bible to know Him, and by knowing Him we will develop the ear of the Spirit. Our primary objective should not be to know the Scriptures but to know the heart of God revealed in the Scriptures. God will reveal Himself to us with His Word. Hosea 4:6 says that God's people "are destroyed for lack of knowledge." Knowledge is information. We know God through the Word. If we do not know God, we will be destroyed.

No other book should take the place of the Bible. Other books are wonderful, and some even give you information about God, but His Word alone is the best source for information that will reveal Him to you.

If you have trouble understanding the Bible, you need to get a translation or version that will break the Word down for you, such as the Amplified, the New International Version or the Living Bible. Meet with someone who has an understanding of the Bible and can help you learn to study it—preferably, a local Bible-teaching church. However, your best and most recommended source for understanding is the Holy Spirit.

Let's look at some basic principles for studying the Word.

There must be a time element involved. We should devote at least an hour a day to pray and read the Word. Jesus asked the disciples to watch and pray for at least an hour. (See Matthew 26:40–41.) All it takes is just one hour a day. If we would all take just 20 minutes to pray, 20 to minutes to read the Word and another 20 minutes to sit and listen to God, that one hour could change our lives forever.

Usually, your mind is freshest when you first wake up. I recommend that you start your day with a fresh Word from God before you attempt to face what lies ahead. It is never good to try to read or attempt to understand the Bible when you are tired. It is difficult to comprehend when you are tired. If morning does not work for you, try taking a nap when you come home in the evenings and then study. This gives you a chance to clear your mind.

Read your Bible and allow God to talk with you directly through the Bible. This works really well when you give

Him first chance at your ears in the morning and write down everything He tells you along with the date. It also goes a long way in helping you to develop your spiritual ear. Since God is the One who gives knowledge of witty inventions, you need to listen for those innovations. God is wisdom, and wisdom will talk to you and tell you things that no one else will tell you. However, we have to train our ears to hear, and the only way to develop your ear is to get quiet before God and listen.

Read prayerfully. We learn how to pray by reading prayerfully. Don't just jump into the Word. Read with a prayerful heart. Ask God to reveal the Word to you. When He sees that you really want to know and you are really hungry for the revelation, He will give it to you. Read thoughtfully. One thought from God can turn a whole world around.

Often times when you are reading the Bible it seems as though one particular scripture or passage jumps out, so don't let that get away from you. Other times as you are reading there is a thought that keeps gnawing at you. Take that thought and write it down. That is a good indication that there is something that God wants to reveal to you. It would be to your advantage to search for scriptures that relate to that thought for more insight. Pray over it. Meditate on it. Pray in tongues over it. Do all you can to see what God is saying to you about that thought or passage. *Write it down!*

Meditate on what you read. This means to ponder what you have read or mutter over it. Another word for this is to *ruminate* on it or chew on it. The more you chew on it, the richer you will be. You can rest assured that if you spend the whole day meditating on the Word you have read or the thought God gives you regarding the Word, blessings will come out of it.

Read obediently. As the truth appeals to your conscience, let it change the habits in your life. Once God reveals Himself or something in the Word to you, let it change your life. Remember, faith without works is dead. While hearing is important, you must also become a *doer* of the Word.

Step 2: Developing a Hearing Ear
Now that we have learned a bit more about the Word, its relationship to God Himself and the importance it plays in the listening side of prayer, let's dig into the meat of how to develop your spiritual ear.

> The thief cometh not, but for to steal, and to kill, and to destroy: I am come that they might have life, and that they might have it more abundantly.
>
> —JOHN 10:10

In 1 Corinthians 3:21 we are told,

> Therefore let no man glory in men. For all things are Yours;

These are very profound statements made by Jesus. He tells us that God wants us to have an abundance of all the things of God. We should have abundant joy, peace, love, faith, finances, health—everything. But the devil comes to steal your abundance. And he will steal it if you do not know the Word, or if you do not take time to hear from God. Remember, Jesus said that His sole purpose in coming was to make it possible for you to have that abundance in all the things that represent God.

> I am the Good Shepherd: the Good

Shepherd giveth His life for the sheep.
—JOHN 10:11

It is the shepherd's responsibility to provide for the sheep—to lead them to pasture, water and shelter. This is what David meant in Psalm 23 when He spoke of the Lord as his Shepherd. He said the Lord would lead him into "green pastures," (pastures that will make us fat, for God knows where our blessings are) and He would also lead him "beside the still waters."

Jesus said He was the "Good Shepherd," so we know that He will do no less than a natural shepherd would. In John 10:27 He even tells us that we as His sheep will hear His voice; He will recognize or know us and we would follow Him. Because we know and hear His voice we will follow Him, and He will lead us to the green pastures and the still waters.

Natural sheep follow the shepherd. They do not try to give him their opinion or tell him what they want or do not want to do. They simply follow the shepherd because they know that he provides for them, protects them and will do them no harm. As spiritual sheep, we too have this blessed assurance. Psalm 23 tells us that "The Lord is my shepherd, I shall not want." God as our Shepherd will not forsake us. He will always provide for us by leading us to the green pastures and still waters, *if we learn to hear* His voice and obey. You do not have to want for anything or lack in any way, because the Shepherd knows where everything we need is and will lead us to it.

Throughout the Word of God, we are given promises from God and His will for us. However, many of us do not know the promises and we do not have a relationship with the God that made them. Therefore, we are not confident in God. And where there's no confidence, it is easy to grow weary and wander off course. But Isaiah 40:28–31 assures us that God is the everlasting God who does not faint, get weary and will strengthen us not to faint.

> Hast thou not known? hast thou not heard, that the everlasting God, the LORD, the Creator of the ends of the earth, fainteth not, neither is weary? there is no searching of His understanding. He giveth power to the faint; and to them that have no might he increaseth strength. Even the youths shall faint and be weary, and the young men shall utterly fall: But they that wait upon the LORD shall renew their strength; they shall mount up with wings as eagles; they shall run, and not be weary; and they shall walk, and not faint.

There is something about a person who knows he has have heard from God; it gives him confidence. You cannot beat a person who is full of confidence.

When you "know that you know that you know" that you have heard from God, it will instill within you strength, confidence and all the things you need to make you successful in life. But if you're wondering whether or not you have heard from God, there will be a certain degree of fear, doubt or unbelief. You will question who's voice it was: yours, God's or the devil's. That is why it is so important for you to learn to hear God's voice and be able to distinguish it from all others. When you know the voice of God, nothing will be able to stand before you, come against you, stop you or turn you away from what He tells you to do. You will have all the confidence and ability you need to take you above any situation.

OLD TESTAMENT EXAMPLES

There are three Old Testament characters that are particularly mentioned as being mighty in prayer and listening. These three examples played a major part in Israel's history. Let's look at their lives and find out what was so special about these three men.

As we study the lives of these men, you will notice several traits that they had in common.

First of all, they were listeners to God's voice. Second, their ears were trained early and over an extended period of time. They were patient during their training until acuteness and sensitivity to God's voice were highly developed.

We all want to be acute and sensitive to the voice of God because it is our sensitivity of heart that will determine what God is able to do in our lives.

Third, they came to the point where they would not move until they heard from God. When you study their lives, their greatest downfalls or times of testing came when they were disobedient to the voice of God. When they strayed, God dealt with their sin and they learned that disobedience had a high price attached to it. And last but not least, in walking with God they learned that the safest place in the world is being in the will of God.

Moses: Two Stages of Training

Our first example is Moses. Moses was the maker and molder of the nation of Israel. Moses was a mighty man of God. There were two distinct stages in the training of Moses' ears where we can glean some great truths.

Stage One: Solitude

First, there were the forty years of solitude in the desert

sands with nothing but sheep, the stars and God. (See Exodus 2.) He had an advantage that many of us do not have today because he was able to get away from it all with no one around him.

We think we must always have people around us. We get down and out and give in to the spirit of loneliness instead of taking advantage of the time alone to hear from God.

During this time alone, Moses' ears were being trained by silence. The confusion of Egypt was being taken out of Moses during his forty years in the desert. All that he had learned to hear in the natural was being weeded out of him–Pharaoh's voice and his way of thinking; the former training he received, along with all of the follies of the world that he had been exposed to at one time or another. God pulled him aside to teach him silence so that He could train and equip him to hear what He wanted him to hear. He wanted Moses to become attuned to the fine, quiet voice of the Spirit.

One of the greatest lessons on hearing from God is the lesson of silence. Few men are strong enough to be able to endure silence. For most of us, the flesh has been in control for so long that we just feel that we have to say something. But in Psalm 4:4 the Bible tells us to " . . . commune with your own heart upon your bed, and be still." Then it even goes a step further and tells says " . . . Selah," which means to meditate on or carefully consider what you just read.

You should lay upon your bed from time to time and just get quiet before God and commune with your heart. *Do not fall asleep and dream*, but be still and listen attentively. When God shares things with you during this time, you need to write them down. You do not have to tell everyone what you heard. It is between you and God. You do not even necessarily need to act on what you hear the first time. Keep bathing in prayer what you hear. If it is truly God, it will stay with you. If it is the devil, it will eventually leave you alone.

Try it. Just for a moment, practice being silent before the Lord. It is not as easy as you may think. For thirty minutes, sit still before God and purpose in your heart not to say anything to Him. With all your heart, listen and be still before Him. Tell Him that you are not going to say anything and that you only want to hear from Him. Then see what happens. If thirty minutes does not work, try fifteen minutes. Remember, Moses had to be pulled away from everything, and if you want this to work for you, you have to do the same, even if only for fifteen minutes. If possible, let your family know what you are doing so that they can respect this time. Or, if necessary, go somewhere where you will not be disturbed. Practice this every day. Give God fifteen to thirty minutes every day where you allow Him to do all the talking. Surely if Moses could give God all day every day for forty years, we can manage fifteen to thirty minutes every day. This could be the greatest time investment you will ever make.

If you are married, you may want to practice this with your spouse. Both of you could come together to hear from God on a decision you need to make. You could get on one side of the bed, while your spouse gets on the other. What will really bless you is when God tells each of you the same thing! Then you can move out in unity knowing that you both heard from God on the matter. And you can bet where there is agreement, God's blessings will be on it. Even if you feel that you have heard from God and your spouse is not in agreement with it, do not move. Ask God to speak to him or her. Get quiet and turn it over to God. You cannot force God's will down another person's throat. But when you move out in unity, God will begin to move on your behalf. (See Amos 3:3 and Psalm 133.)

Make this confession with me to hear what the Spirit of the Lord is saying. Stick your fingers in your ears. Now say this: I must hear from God. Anoint my ears to hear, Lord Jesus. Anoint my ears to hear Your precious Spirit, and I will develop the ear to hear.

Stage Two: Pulling Away to Listen

Moses' second stage was followed by eighty days of listening to God's spoken voice on the mountain. Twice after God used him to bring His people out of Egypt, Moses was pulled away to spend time in the presence of the Almighty for forty days and forty nights (Exodus 24:18; 34:28). Now if you have done the experiment suggested earlier, you have a small glimpse of what Moses experienced during those forty days and nights. Can you imagine what God was able to do in his life during those forty days and nights? He became so full of the power of God and had such an anointing upon him that the people could not even look him in the face. They had to put a veil over his face so that the people could look at him!

LESSONS TO BE LEARNED

We can learn some great things from the previous example. The anointing comes from spending time in the presence of God—not talking to anyone else, but just spending time in His presence, learning to hear His voice. Accomplishing great things for God comes from spending time alone with Him. You must hear His will, listen to His orders and then be obedient to follow through on them. We have to pull ourselves away from everything—the hustle, bustle and business of life—we are familiar with in order to hear God. Moses delighted in his time alone with God. It was an opportunity to commune with Him, learn from Him and get divine instruction. The Bible tells us in Psalm 37:4, "delight thyself also in the Lord and He shall give thee the desires of thine heart." When you spend time alone in the presence of God on a continual basis, the desires of your heart are the desires of His heart. You will not want anything that He does not want for you. Your will becomes His will and your thoughts become His thoughts.

Say this: Thank God that I hear His voice! Thank God I hear His voice! Thank God I hear His voice. I hear from God and I obey His will for my life just as Moses did in the cleft of the mountain. *My life is not built around what others say about me but what God says about me and to me!*

Samuel

Our next Old Testament example is Samuel. Samuel's life is a little different from Moses'. Samuel was the patient teacher who introduced a new order of things into the national life of Israel. What made his life so different? First of all, he had a mother that loved God dearly. She was found in the temple praying daily for a man-child. As a matter of fact, she got so caught up in the Spirit, that Eli thought she was drunk. (See 1 Samuel 1:11–15.)

She made a promise, a vow to God, that if He gave her a son she would give him back to God. While yet a child, before his ears had been dulled by worldly sounds, Samuel's ears were tuned to hearing the voice of God.

How did this happen? Hannah, his mother, turned Samuel over to God as a child. He did not have to go through forty years of being trained like Moses did. God did not have to pull him aside to get all of the world's ways out of him. Samuel was brought up ministering in the house of God. Like a lot of Christians, he was being trained at an early age. However, unlike many Christians, he did not depart from his teaching as he grew older. His ears were quickly trained to recognize God's voice.

And the child Samuel ministered unto the LORD before Eli. And the word of the LORD was precious in those days; there was no open vision. And it came to pass at that time, when Eli was laid down in his place, and his eyes began to wax dim, that he could not see; And ere the lamp of God went out in the temple of the LORD, where the ark of God was, and Samuel was laid down to sleep; That the LORD called Samuel: and he answered, Here am I. And he ran unto Eli, and said, Here am I; for thou calledst me. And he said, I called not; lie down again. And he went and lay down. And the LORD called yet again, Samuel. And Samuel arose and went to Eli, and said, Here am I; for thou didst call me. And he answered, I called not, my son; lie down again. Now Samuel did not yet know the LORD, neither was the word of the LORD yet revealed unto him. And the LORD called Samuel again the third time. And he arose and went to Eli, and said, Here am I; for thou didst call me. And Eli perceived that the LORD had called the child. Therefore Eli said unto Samuel, Go, lie down: and it shall be, if he call thee, that thou shalt say, Speak, LORD; for thy servant heareth. So Samuel went and lay down in his place. And the LORD came, and stood, and called as at other times, Samuel, Samuel.

Then Samuel answered, Speak; for thy servant heareth.

—1 SAMUEL 3:1–10

Because Samuel did not had not yet developed the ear to hear the voice of the Lord, he ran to the man of God, just like many of us do who do not know God's voice.

Just as with Moses and with us, Samuel's ears had to be trained to hear from God. There are many voices that speak to people, but you have to try the spirits by the Spirit (1 John 4:1). That is why the Word of the Lord tries everything. People who know God hear His Word. The voice we should listen to is the One that is always in line with God's Word.

Understand beloved, God will never tell you anything contrary to His Word. That is why when you come to a truly righteous man or woman of God and ask them about something, they will only tell you what the Word says if they tell you anything at all. Often, it may not be what your flesh wants to hear. However, they know that as people of God, their responsibility is to only say what the Word says. It is their job to always bring the perfect will of God to your life. Everything that they teach, counsel or show you is for this purpose and this purpose only.

Elijah

Let's look at our third Old Testament example, Elijah. Elijah was a bit more rugged than Samuel. He was the leader God used when the national worship of Jehovah was about to be overthrown. We can learn several things from Elijah. The Word of the Lord came to Elijah as the result of constant praying, listening and watching on the mountaintop.

Now remember, God called Moses to the wilderness

for forty years to get the ways of Egypt out of him and then twice He pulled Moses aside for forty days and forty nights so that He could talk to him. Samuel was introduced to God at an early age but it was a while before he actually learned the voice of God. Elijah, on the other hand, had to be in persistent prayer to be able to bring forth the Word of the Lord. In Ephesians 6:18 and 2 Timothy 1:3, the Bible tells us about praying with all perseverance. Just as with Elijah, if we really want to develop a listening ear, one of the things we are going to have to do is to persevere to enter in to where you are hearing from God. You must understand that Satan will fight you all of the days of your life to keep you from hearing from God. He knows that the day you begin listening to God and practice hearing from God is when you are really going to be blessed. He does not have the power to stop you if God can get you to listen to His voice and obey.

Notice that the Word of the Lord came to Elijah in 1 Kings 18 just it came to Samuel in 1 Samuel 3. When the Word of the Lord comes to you, will you be in a position to hear? Will you be silent long enough to hear the Word of the Lord? Are you willing to not speak or move until you hear from God regarding your situation? Will you be obedient to the Holy Spirit? Are you fighting against the Holy Spirit or yielding to Him?

When the Word of the Lord came to Elijah, it gave him a spirit of boldness. He was so tuned in to the voice of God that he obeyed God at all costs. He did not even have the Holy Spirit living on the inside of him as we do today. Yet, he did what the Lord instructed him to do even though he could have been killed. He became so confident in what God told him that he made a mockery of the devil. Elijah came in and challenged Jezebel and four hundred and fifty prophets of Baal.

In 1 Kings chapter 18 the Word of the Lord came to Elijah that it was going to rain. Now mind you, it had not rained in more than three years. Of course people thought he was crazy because there were no signs of rain, not even a cloud in the sky. But in spite of all this, Elijah believed the word he heard from the Lord. He challenged the people of God as well as the enemy based upon what he heard. He mocked the enemy and made a fool of them.

Now you have got to be pretty confident that you hear from God in order to mock the devil and four hundred and fifty of his prophets!

Elijah heard the sound of the abundance of rain even though there was no sign of rain. (See 1 Kings 18:41.) From where did he get that? In verse 1, the Word of the Lord came to Elijah that it was going to rain. Elijah believed the word he heard and spoke it to others, even though he had to send his servant to look for the rain cloud *seven times* before he saw a cloud the size of a man's hand. Now that type of cloud would not mean much to some people, but because Elijah was looking for something from God, he knew beyond a shadow of a doubt that it would rain just as God said it would. He persisted in praying and sending forth the servant to see the manifestation of the Word of the Lord. He did not let the tangible affect what he heard by the Spirit. And lo, that little cloud covered the sky and the sky became dark and God brought forth a great rain. (See 1 Kings 18:41–45.) That's pretty bold confidence!

It is important to note that Elijah had both the ear of the Spirit and the eye of the Spirit. Once he knew that he had heard from God, he began looking for God to bring His word to pass.

If you do not look for the blessings that God speaks to you about, they will never come. God will only show

Himself to those that look for and expect Him. (See 2 Peter 3:11–14.)

Once you have heard from God, at no time should you let circumstances and evidence that is contrary to what you have heard stop you from looking for God to bring it to pass. You must be persistent! You have to break through and keep praying and believing. Know beyond a shadow of a doubt that if God said it, He'll do it and if He spoke it, He will bring it to pass! Once you know that you have heard from God, you must maintain your faith! At no time should you let opposition stop you from believing what God has told you. Satan will send opposition to get you not to trust the Word and the voice of God, but you must have faith against all opposition.

Again, let me remind you that in order to develop a listening ear, you have got to learn to get away from the familiar, the noise and the business, and get silent before God in order to hear His still small voice. There is a praying time, but there is also a time to be silent and listen.

Old Testament Keys

Now before we move on, let's review the lessons we have learned from these three men in the Old Testament.

1. The Word of the Lord comes when we get quiet before Him.
2. In order to hear from God, we often have to pull ourselves away from what we think we know. This can be from religion/church versus what the Word of God teaches us.
3. It takes training and perseverance to develop an ear to hear God.
4. Once we know that we have heard from God, we have to lay claim to what we have heard and

know and anticipate that the devil will send opposition to what God has told us.

5. We have to look for God to manifest what he speaks to us. We have to stand fast in believing that if He said it, He will do it; and if He spoke it, He will bring it to pass. In spite of what we see or hear in the natural, we have to proclaim what we have heard and look for it to come to pass. That's called seeing things with the eye of the Spirit.

6. What we see and what we hear by the Spirit will determine how far we are going to go with God.

Jesus: Our New Testament Example

Of course we all know that Jesus is always our greatest example in all things. He came into the earth as a man to show us what could be done in the spirit, and He expects us to do even greater things than He did. (See John 14:12.) Now in order for us to accomplish this, don't you think we need to take a look at how He was so successful in the things He did?

Jesus would not speak until He heard from the Father. He, of course, had the tongue of the learned. This is what made His life so different from all the other men on the earth. People were amazed at His authority and ability to handle any situation. Why? Because He did not speak as a natural man, He spoke only under the unction of the Holy Spirit. At times when Jesus was confronted, He would not say a single word. Now you know that bothered Satan because he could not get Him to talk. But in a lot of situations, Jesus would not say anything because He knew that He should not and dared not until He heard from His Father.

Simply said, if the Father would not say anything, Jesus would not say anything. The religious leaders tried to get Jesus to say just one wrong thing. More than likely, they would have tried to judge His every word so that they could find fault in Him, but He would only speak what the Word said or what the Spirit led Him to say. Therefore, they could find no fault in Him.

Can you imagine how powerful we could be if we learned this one characteristic of Jesus? Just imagine if someone said something to provoke us, and we just remained quite until we heard the Holy Spirit say something.

I bet we would have a lot fewer divorces if we learned this principle. No matter which of the two spouses would get upset, the other one would just sit through it quietly and only say what the Holy Spirit leads them to say (which in most cases is nothing!)

Now on the other hand, our tongues will probably want to rebel. While the Holy Spirit is telling us to be quiet, our tongues are saying "I cannot be quiet! I cannot be quiet!" Then it comes down to who we are going to obey—the flesh (our tongues in this case) or the Spirit. We have a choice. But bear in mind John 8:47, "He that is of God heareth God's words: ye therefore hear them not, because ye are not of God." Remember God's Word has a solution for every situation. He will speak that Word to us, but it is up to us whether or not we are going to do it. We should also remember that it takes two people to argue.

FOLLOWING HIS EXAMPLE

We need to follow the example of Jesus. In John 8:28, Jesus stated that He did and said nothing in and of Himself, but only did as His Father did and spoke. The only way that we are going to be able to follow His example is to develop our spiritual ears and eyes so that we can hear and see what Father God desires for us.

Let us become " . . .swift to hear, slow to speak, slow to wrath" (James 1:19). Purpose in your heart not to speak until you hear from God. Do not respond until you know what God would say. This is what is called *true order: first* hearing from God and *then* hearing from man. Not hearing from man first and then hearing from God. True order produces tremendous results.

> *Prayer: Father, we thank You and praise You for anointing our ears to hear Your voice, that we may have the tongue of the learned and the ear of the Spirit. Thank You, Lord, that You will lead us and guide us in all manner of truth. And we will forever give You the praise, the honor and the glory. Anoint our hearts along with our ears, that we may continually walk out Your divine will. Jesus, build Your character in us that we may be like You in everything. Teach us to be quiet. Teach us to be still. Teach us all to be silent that we may practice hearing Your voice speaking to our spirit. In Jesus' name we pray, amen.*

Chapter Five

Your Actual Training

Developing a listening ear to train ourselves to hear the voice of God is not something that you learn overnight. It takes time . . . a lifetime. This type of development never stops. You never come to the point where you can say that you have learned all there is to know about hearing from God. No matter how long you have walked with God and had a relationship with Him, there is always something new to learn.

TRAINING OUR EARS

One of the first things you need to do is to practice waiting on Him. The practice of waiting on God is a form of obedience that requires a great deal of patience.

When we pray we are looking for answers. Therefore, prayer must be a conversation, not a dissertation. If you want to hear God's part of the conversation, you will have to learn to be patient and listen. You cannot just run to Him and expect to do all of the talking and not allow Him to speak to you. The wise man spends time in His presence and waits to hear from Him. Remember in Isaiah 40:31 we learned that " . . . they that wait upon the LORD shall renew their strength; they shall mount up with wings as eagles; they shall run, and not be weary; and they shall walk, and not faint."

Now if waiting on God is a form of obedience, then you have probably already guessed that not waiting on Him is a form of rebellion.

> . . .this is a rebellious people, lying children, children that will not hear the law of the Lord.
> —Isaiah 30:9

In this scripture, God is talking about the children of Israel. He called them "a rebellious people" because they would not stop and hear the law of the Lord and obey it. The children of Israel did not have the opportunity to actually hear the voice of God as we do today. God's prophets were used to telling them what God wanted them to know. They only had the written Word. Very seldom did people actually hear the voice of God. But as we learned earlier, Jesus came that we would have a more abundant life than the people in the Old Testament. He also sent the Holy Spirit so that we would have a direct connection to speak to and hear from God here on the earth.

> Wherefore thus saith the Holy One of Israel, Because ye despise this word, [the Word of God] and trust in oppression and perverseness, and stay thereon: Therefore this iniquity shall be to you as a breach ready to fall, swelling out in a high wall, whose breaking cometh suddenly at an instant.
> —Isaiah 30:12–13

When you are not patient to take the time to listen to God, Satan will capitalize on your ignorance of the Word and how the Spirit of God would have you to respond to a particular situation. Those who do not take time to listen to God and read and obey His Word are acting upon what they think they know (or their own natural perception) instead of the Wisdom of God.

God says that "My people are destroyed for lack of knowledge" (Hosea 4:6). We have a lack of knowledge because we do not stop long enough to see what the Scriptures say about our situation or take the time to listen so that God can instruct us. Whatever the Word says, that should be our final authority. Whether it is forgiving or trusting Him or any other command, we must obey the Word. We cannot expect God to manifest Himself on our behalf or bless us if we disobey His Word.

PUTTING GOD FIRST

God must be first—even over cleaning the house and all of your other responsibilities. Let God look into your heart. Let Him see that He is first. What was the first commandment Jesus gave? To ". . . love the Lord thy God with all of thy heart, and with all thy soul, and with all thy mind" (Matt. 22:37). When God looks into a heart and sees a heart that is willing to put Him first over the business, the family, the church and over everything else, it is pleasing to Him. God will not play second fiddle to anything or anyone. He knows that you have responsibilities. He knows that these things are important. But He must know, above all things, that He is first! He must be the most important thing in your life, and pleasing Him must be your number one priority. Once you please God, He will take care of the rest. Remember Jesus said, " . . . seek ye first the Kingdom of God and His righteousness and all these things shall be added unto you" (Matt. 6:33). God will take care of the "things."

"If ye then be risen with Christ, seek those things which are above, . . . Set your affections on those things above, not on things on the earth" (Col. 3:1–2). When you put God first and yearn for Him, you will tap into a special place in God. You will become dead to "things." You will have one desire, and that will be to know God. Your affections will be above, not upon the earth. You will be dead to the things of the world. All you will want is Jesus and to hear from Him. Pleasing Him will be all you need in order to be satisfied.

Know in your heart that God will not hide Himself from you when you seek Him with all of your heart. He will be there for you even when your mother and father have forsaken you. He will teach you His ways and lead you on a plain path so that your enemy will not overtake you. But you must believe that you will see the goodness of the Lord! You must wait, hope for, and expect Him. Be of good courage, for He will strengthen your heart! Faint not, for your strength comes from the Lord, and your confidence comes when you get quiet to hear from Him. (See Psalm 27:7–14.)

> . . . in Him we live, and move, and have our being.
> —Acts 17:28

> As ye have therefore received Christ Jesus the Lord, so walk ye in Him: Rooted and built up in Him, and stablished in the faith, as ye have been taught, abounding therein with thanksgiving.
> —Colossians 2:6–7

The most important thing that life has to offer is pleasing God. If you make pleasing God and putting Him first the number one thing in your life, you too will be blessed like David and all the others in the Bible that God poured His blessings upon. No matter where you search in the Word, you will not be able to find one reference where a person put God first, and God did not provide for him. He wants you to prosper. In 3 John 2 He tells us that, "Beloved, I wish above all things that thou mayest prosper and be in health, even as thy soul prospereth." But He wants your soul to prosper first, and the only way for your soul to prosper is for you to put Him first. Only then can you live and abide in Him and let Him live and abide in you.

WAITING

> For thus saith the Lord God, the Holy One of Israel; In returning and rest shall ye be saved; in quietness and in confidence shall be your strength . . .
>
> —ISAIAH 30:15

In this passage of scripture, the word *rest* means "peace." When a person is at peace, they are often quiet or tranquil. When you are quiet and peaceful, you can hear from God. Knowing that you have heard from God brings confidence; quietness and confidence will be your strength in times of trouble. "But they that wait upon the LORD shall renew their strength . . ." (Isa. 40:31).

So in quietness, wait for God; get before Him with an ear to hear Him. Once He has spoken to you, have confidence in what you know He has spoken to you. Then you shall be strengthened. When you allow God the proper time to speak back to your heart, and you know beyond a shadow of a doubt that you have heard from Him, you will be confident. In 1 John 5:14–15, John said " . . .this is the confidence that we have in Him, that, if we ask any thing according to His will, He hearth us: And . . . we know that we have the petitions that we desired of Him."

The Rewards of Waiting . . .His Promise of Blessings

> And therefore will the LORD wait, that He may be gracious unto you, and therefore will He be exalted, that He may have mercy upon you: for the LORD is a God of judgement: blessed are all they that wait for Him.
>
> —ISAIAH 30:18

Remember, blessed are all of those that will take time to wait upon the Lord. And for those that wait upon the Lord, He promises to renew their strength in quietness and confidence. (See Isaiah 40.)

The Fat of the Land . . .

> Then shall he give the rain of thy seed, that thou shalt sow the ground withal; and bread of the increase of the earth, and it shall be fat and plenteous: in that day shall thy cattle feed in large pastures.
>
> —ISAIAH 30:23

When we wait to hear from God and obey what He says, everything we have will be fat! We will eat the fat of the land! That's right, we will eat the fat of the land because our Good Shepherd knows where the fat of the land is located. He, as our Good Shepherd, knows what will make us fat and how to get it to us. It is our responsibility to learn to listen that He might lead us and direct us to the good of the land. "If ye be willing and obedient, ye shall eat the good [or the fat] of the land" (Isa. 1:19). The key is *listening and obeying.* This is the only way that God will cause you to eat the good or the fat of the land.

The Destruction of Our Enemies . . .

> For through the voice of the LORD shall the Assyrian [or enemy] be beaten down, which smote with a rod.
>
> —ISAIAH 30:31

Through the voice of the Lord, your enemies will be destroyed if you practice listening and obeying. Your enemies will be smitten, knocked down and made to be your footstool when you practice hearing from God. David said, "A thousand shall fall at thy side, and ten thousand at thy right hand; but it shall not come nigh thee" (Ps. 91:7).

GETTING QUIET TO HEAR FROM GOD

You must take time to develop a quiet spirit. It is not as easy as you may think. Trying to get quiet before God takes diligence. Do you remember the assignment that I gave you earlier? I asked you to try to be quiet for a short amount of time. Do you remember the noise of the world, all the things you suddenly heard that you may not have paid any attention to before? Do you remember how many times the telephone rang or a family member or friend interrupted you? These are the things of the world that the enemy uses to try to crowd out the still, small voice. But you cannot give up. Remember, it took God forty years to rid Moses of the noise of Egypt. Moses only had the sheep to talk to all that time, and it helped him to develop an ear to hear God. (See Exodus 2.) It also took forty years of wandering in the desert before the murmuring and complaining noise stopped with the children of Israel. There is a lot of noise in your life that you must tune out and eliminate before you are able to hear that quiet, still, small voice of God.

> Be still, and know that I am God: I will be exalted among the heathen, I will be exalted in the earth.
>
> —PSALM 46:10

It is important not to come before God and shout out everything you have on your mind. You must learn to be quiet before Him and know that He is God. Notice what He said in verse 11 of that same chapter, "The Lord of hosts is with us; the God of Jacob is our refuge. Selah." [Think on this; meditate on this; chew on this and just be quiet and know that He is God.]

If you were to just meditate on these two scriptures alone you could defeat the devil. You get your strength when you get quiet before the Lord and meditate on Him. He can then give you direction. And once you get direction from God, the devil better not get in your way, because if he does, you'll just run over him.

> Stand in awe, and sin not: commune with your own heart upon your bed, and be still. Selah. [meditate on this, think on this and give place to this].
>
> —PSALM 4:4

If you are practicing sin, then you are not hearing from

God. The Bible says ". . . God heareth not sinners: but if any man be a worshipper of God, and doeth his will, him he heareth" (John 9:31). You cannot truly worship God with a mess in your life. When you have sin in your life, the fellowship with God is broken. Mind you, I did not say the *relationship* is broken, but the *fellowship* is broken. If there is no fellowship, there is no communication. The fellowship cannot pick up again until you repent before God and get your life back in order. For the Bible says, "if I regard iniquity in my heart, the Lord will not hear me" (Ps. 66:18). Therefore, we must be quick to forgive and ask God's forgiveness when we sin and others sin against us.

TAKING TIME TO MINISTER TO THE LORD

One of the best things you can do while you wait is to practice *becoming more concerned about worshipping Him and being in His presence.* Take time just for Him.

When most people think of worshipping God, they immediately think of worship in the church. Many of us learned worship from the church. This type of corporate worship brings unity and harmony in the Spirit, which brings forth the blessings of God.

But it stands to reason that, if corporate church worship will bring unity and harmony, the same would be true in our personal lives. When we personally take time to worship the Lord, it unites us with the Holy Spirit and the angels in heaven, which brings unity and harmony into our personal lives and relationship with God. (See Revelation 5:10–13.) So let's look at unity and harmony. It will help us to learn a bit more about our personal worship and ministry unto God.

It came even to pass, as the TRUMPETERS

AND SINGERS WERE AS ONE, [notice the importance of maintaining unity, especially husbands and wives as they go before God] to make ONE SOUND to be heard in praising and thanking the LORD; and WHEN THEY LIFTED UP THEIR VOICE [one voice in unity] with the trumpets and cymbals and instruments of musick, and praised the LORD, saying, For He is good; for His mercy endureth for ever: that then the house was filled with a cloud, even the house of the Lord; So that the priests could not stand to minister by reason of the cloud: for the glory of the LORD had filled the house of God.
—2 CHRONICLES 5:13–14, EMPHASIS ADDED

As believers it is very important that we learn to walk in unity and harmony. We—especially husbands and wives and church members—are called to walk together as one. We cannot hear from God when there is not a united front. Therefore, if you are not willing to forgive and walk in love, you cannot hear from God. It blocks communication from God to your heart. (Refer to the section in Chapter three. It specifically deals with the importance of the condition of your heart and hearing from God.)

Disharmony stems from obeying your flesh and doing what you think rather than obeying the voice of God. Flesh will draw you away from God. When we are united together in one accord, worshipping God together (praising God with one heart and one spirit), the glory of the Lord will come in. You never know when the glory cloud will come. As shown in previously mentioned scriptures, the people had come together to worship God and praise Him. They truly had one heart and one voice crying unto Him with such strong unity that the glory cloud of the Lord came in and sat right upon them. As a matter of fact, the cloud was so great that the priests could not stand to minister.

The church today could stand to have a few services like that, and we can when we do the same thing these people did. They came with an ear to hear, in one accord, in whatever manner the Spirit of God was leading, and joined forces. They did not try to do things their own way—they followed the Spirit. They yielded to Him and united together in one accord.

Throughout the Bible we see example after example of how God blessed the people when they were unified. Remember Psalm 133:1 and 3, "Behold, how good and how pleasant it is for brethren to dwell together in unity! . . . the Lord commanded the blessing, even life for evermore." In Acts 2 when the disciples were one in the upper room (in one accord, in one place), the Holy Spirit came.

The only time that God will command His blessings and pour out His blessings is when people are united and moving in one accord. Look at Genesis 11:6, "And the LORD said, Behold, the people is one, and they have all one language; and this they begin to do: and now nothing will be restrained from them, which they have imagined to do." God said that because the people were one—with one language and one mind—there was nothing that they imagined to do that they could not have accomplished. If this was what was possible with the children of men, how much more should be done and accomplished through the children of God? In Psalm 22:3 it speaks of God abiding in the praises of His people. When the people are one, moving and flowing in the Spirit of God, it is beautiful to God and He will bless it. Harmony, unity and people flowing together in marriage, in the church, as a team or group set out to do the work of the Lord is beautiful in the sight of God and it causes His blessings to flow.

We must bear in mind that the devil is the author of confusion. He is the one that sows discord and separates people, because he knows that as long as the people are separated it hinders the blessings of God. When people are not in one accord, you can rest assured that they are not hearing from God. When people walk around with chips on their shoulders, mad at the world and walking in unforgiveness, they are not hearing from God.

In Acts 13 we are told about the prophets and teachers coming together in one accord to minister to the Lord. In verse 2 we read: "As they ministered to the Lord and fasted, the Holy Ghost said, Separate me Barnabas and Saul for the work whereunto I have called them." Notice, as they ministered to the Lord and fasted, they were able to get directions from God by the Holy Spirit for their ministry and for their lives. We must take time to minister to God always. As we do so, He will take time to minister to us and give us a word and direction for our situations.

SPENDING TIME IN THE PRESENCE OF GOD

Most great men that really went on to do great things for God spent an enormous amount of time ministering to God and spending time in His presence. They took time to hear from God; to wait upon Him; to look for Him in every situation. They developed a hearing ear and did not hesitate getting before God. As a result, they developed the strength in the Lord that they needed to do the great things God called them to do. They took to heart the words "they that wait upon the LORD shall renew their strength . . ." (Isa. 40:31). And by His strength, they were able to do things that they could not do in the natural. For as the Word says in Philippians 4:13, "I can do all things through Christ which strengtheneth me." As people of God, we too are destined for greatness, but greatness requires ministering to God, spending time in His presence and having a hearing ear. We cannot do the will of the Father in the strength of a man.

BEING TOO BUSY TO HEAR

Is God pleased with what you are doing? Are you spending enough quality time with Him? Are you spending time ministering to Him? Are you developing a listening ear for God the Father? When people develop a listening ear for God and obey Him it is pleasing to Him. It is the Father's good pleasure to give unto them the Kingdom of God. (See Luke 12:32.)

The one thing that Satan tries to do to hinder our walk with God and our greatness in Him is to make us so busy that we forget to spend time ministering to God and waiting upon Him. One thing I have learned is when you are too busy to spend quality time with God, you are too busy to live. Even being too involved in church activities and not spending the proper time with God and hearing from Him is dangerous. We need to study our lives, prioritize our lives and make sure that what we are doing is not so important that we do not have time for God. Our number one priority should be spending the proper time in the presence of the Lord. There are a lot of things that one can do in life that are good in one sense, but the most important thing you can do is to take time to minister to God and get quiet before Him.

Now it came to pass, as they went, that He [Jesus] went into a certain village: and a certain woman named Martha received Him into her house. And she had a sister called Mary, which also sat at Jesus' feet, and heard His word. But Martha was cumbered about much serving, and came to Him, and said, Lord, dost Thou not care that my sister hath left me to serve alone? bid her therefore that she help me. And Jesus answered and said unto her, Martha, Martha, thou art careful and troubled about many things: But one thing is needful: and Mary hath chosen that good part, which shall not be taken away from her.

—LUKE 10:38–42

This scripture is not intended to give you an excuse to allow your house to get dirty or not take care of what God has blessed you with. However, there is a time and a place for everything. Martha's cleaning of her house at this particular time was not the appropriate thing to do. On the other hand, Mary realized that the best thing, the most appropriate thing for her to do, was to minister to the Lord, to sit at His feet and get quiet so that she could hear Him.

The devil capitalizes on people being too busy to spend time with God. These people allow themselves to get so busy doing things that may be important, but for that particular time or season they are not the most appropriate. The devil tricks them into believing that they do not have time to pray because they have to do the housework or tend to other things. They fail to realize that if they were to spend the proper time with God and take the time to get quiet before Him, they could do all those other things in less time and probably more efficiently!

God knows you have work to do. He knows the things and responsibilities you have before you. All He asks is that you make Him the number one priority. When you do, He'll redeem the time for you and allow you to do all the things you need to get done. You must take time to minister unto the Lord! Nothing is more important than that! In Luke 10:38–42, what Martha was doing was good, but for that particular hour and time, it was not the most important thing for her to do.

As you can see in verse 41, Jesus told Martha that she was careful and troubled, which means: worried, fretful, or anxious, over *many* things. He also told her that the *one* thing that she needed to learn was to spend time in the presence of the Lord. She needed to stop the *busy work* and take time to minister to the Lord, to sit at His feet and hear from Him.

Just like Martha, there are women that are home all day who are so busy with housework that they never take the time to minister to the Lord. They rarely take time to sit at His feet and hear from Him. Therefore, they miss God. And it is not just the women, men miss it too. We are all guilty of getting too caught up in what we call *"earning a living"* instead of spending time with God for direction. Few of us take time to minister to Him, time to wait on Him. Many times we step out doing what we think we ought to do versus what He desires us to do. We fail to realize that the blessings are in our obedience to what He desires us to do, or commands us to do. That is what Jesus meant when He told us in Mark 4:24 to take heed to what we hear. And in Luke 8:18 we are told to be careful how we hear. He is trying to tell us to listen and be obedient. We must crowd out the noise of the world and find out what God is saying about our situation.

Don't move until you are confident that you have heard from God.

Are you ministering to God; spending time with Him;

listening to Him; heeding His voice? Or are you like Martha, so busy doing that you do not take the time to hear from God and sit in His presence? Remember, the work Martha was doing was good, but was it the most important thing for her to do at the time? If you do not actually place a priority on your time with God and studying the Word, the devil will crowd that time out and always put something in its place. He'll keep you so busy that you will *think* you actually do not have time to give to God. And that is his ultimate goal—to get you so busy that you do not take the time to pursue God and His Word.

I know this for a fact. It seems like when it is my meditation time that's when everyone needs to talk to me or needs something from me. The telephone rings, the dog, the cat, and everyone else thinks they need something from me. Why? Because the devil knows that there is nothing more important than me spending time with God and getting quiet before Him. Therefore, I have learned that it is up to me to do whatever it takes to make sure I have uninterrupted time in with God. I turn the telephone off, put a sign on my door and do whatever I have to do. As a matter of fact, have you ever noticed that most of the time the devil will even try to use our own bodies to keep us from spending time with God? You may not be sleepy, but if you start reading your Bible that is when the devil tries to make you think you are too sleepy to read. That is why we have to have a heart that yearns for the listening side of prayer.

Having a Yearning to Hear

And it shall come to pass, if thou shalt hearken diligently unto the voice of the LORD thy God, to observe and to do all His commandments which I command thee this day, that the LORD thy God will set thee on high above all nations of the earth:

—DEUTERONOMY 28:1

The word *hearken* means "to hear with attention or interest; to obey diligently; to give heed to; to listen to; to yield to." If you do not really yearn in your heart to develop a hearing ear, more than likely you will never develop it. The Bible says that he that hungers and thirsts after righteousness shall be filled. (See Luke 6:21.) To hunger and thirst after something means that you *crave it, long for it, desire it, require it or yearn for it.* When you feel this way about something, you are willing to go the extra mile and do whatever it takes to get it. You press in at all costs.

As important as developing the listening side of prayer is for you in your walk with God, if you do not yearn for it in your heart and take the time to develop it, you will not get it. You will more than likely continue in the same steps you have taken in the past and remain where you are. God rewards those who hunger and have a desire to grow in Him. If you have a casual or lax attitude, God will allow you to remain where you are as opposed to where He desires to take you.

Notice what David said in Psalm 119:131,

> I opened my mouth, and panted: for I longed for Thy commandments.

In Acts 13:22 the Word of God tells us that David was a man after God's own heart. If he longed for and panted after God's Word, it would seem to me that we too ought to put God's Word in the proper place in our lives. All throughout Psalm 119 we see how David gave the Word proper place in his life. In Psalm 27:1–4 David says,

> The LORD is my light and my salvation; whom shall I fear? the LORD is the strength of my life; of whom shall I be afraid? When the wicked, even mine enemies and my foes, came upon me to eat up my flesh, they stumbled and fell. Though an host should encamp against me, my heart shall not fear: though war should rise against me, in this will I be confident. One thing have I desired of the LORD, that will I seek after; that I may dwell in the house of the LORD all the days of my life, to behold the beauty of the LORD, and to inquire in His temple.

Once you take time to sit before God and hear from Him, you will not want anything to get in the way of your being with Him. It will give you confidence and strength. You will learn not to fret or fear anything, no matter how much or how many come against you. You will come to the point of knowing that if God be for you, who can be against you? (See Romans 8:31.) When you have heard from God you can rest assured that a thousand may fall at your side, and ten thousand at your right hand but nothing will come near your dwelling. (See Psalm 91:7.) You will not have to worry about the devil once God speaks to you because you will know that God is with you!

Time with God will help you to become like David. You too will develop a longing, thirsting and yearning after Him in your heart. But you must remember, David learned to be still before God and came to the place where he craved God and His Word more than anything. Likewise, Job had such a desire for God and His Word that he wanted it more than he desired food! (See Job 23:12.) That is what God is looking for in our lives and hearts, that we long to know Him and walk in His will regardless of the costs.

> One thing have I desired of the LORD, that will I seek after; that I may dwell in the house of the LORD all the days of my life, to behold the beauty of the LORD, and to inquire in His temple. For in the day of trouble He will hide me in His pavilion: in the secret place of His tent will He hide me; He will set me high upon a rock.
> —PSALM 27:4–5, NKJV

If you know anything about the life of David, you know that God had given him an abundant supply of everything you could imagine: wealth, houses, land and power. But in all that he had, his heart's desire was still to seek after God and dwell in the Lord's house. David tapped into what most people spend a lifetime searching for. He tapped into the heart of God through the listening side of prayer; spending time with God; ministering to God and beholding His beauty.

Just to look upon God's beauty and to enter into His temple is such an awesome privilege. But can you imagine that as a result of your desiring Him, He will hide you in the time of trouble and set you upon His shelter, upon a rock? God wants to reveal His wisdom and knowledge to you. He does not want to hide you so you cannot be seen. He wants to set you up so your enemies can see you and become your footstool, but you must yearn for Him and at all costs put Him first.

Chapter Six

How God Speaks Today

You have learned how to hear from God. Now it is time to learn some of the ways God will speak to you.

HIS WORD

God uses His Word in many different ways to speak to us today.

As you give yourself to reading and studying God's Word, the Lord will speak to you through the Scriptures. When you receive a confirmation from the Scriptures, it's like a Roman candle "going off" inside of you. Nobody will have to tell you that it is God; you will know it.

When we allow it to, the Word of God will wash our minds and cleanse our spirits. As we meditate upon God's Word, it becomes like water, which cleanses and washes. Paul told us in Ephesians 5:25–26 "Christ loved the Church and gave Himself for her, so that He might sanctify her, having cleansed her by the washing of water with the Word" (Author's paraphrase of the Amplified translation). And Jesus said to His disciples, "Now ye clean through the Word which I have spoken unto you" (John 15:3).

God will also use the Word to show you how to defeat the devil. When the devil came to Christ in the wilderness to tempt Him, Jesus did not pray. He did not praise. He did not bind or loose. He spoke the Word of God and Satan retreated. It is the same for us today. God intends for His Word to be one of our offensive weapons against the devil.

There is a word in the Bible for every situation of life. But you must spend time in the Bible in order for God to use it to speak to you. When you spend time in the Word, you come to know it in your heart, not just memorized verses that you recite from time to time, but you form an intimate knowledge and witness to it. Then, like Jesus, when the enemy comes to attack, you too can speak the "it is written" for whatever he tries to use against you. For example, when the enemy comes to me and says, "You are weak," I know that it is written, ". . . let the weak say I am strong" (Joel 3:10). When the devil says, "You are poor," I reply, "Devil, I am rich because of what the Lord has done for me. It is written, 'My God shall supply all of my needs according to His riches in glory by Christ Jesus.' " (See Philippians 4:19.)

Believers who are not well grounded in God's Word may have trouble with the devil planting doubt in their minds. Therefore, you must make a commitment to study the Bible each day, systematically, spiritually and expectantly. As you do, it will help to fine-tune your ears to know and understand the voice of God.

AN INNER IMPRESSION OR INNER WITNESS

An impression is an image. Sometimes God will place an image in your heart. But you must understand that when God speaks, He speaks from the inside because the Holy Spirit lives and dwells on the inside of you.

Before you were born again, you were only taught to receive all of your information from the outside. This is natural. All of your five physical senses deal with the outward man—hearing, seeing, touching, smelling and tasting. But now that you are saved, suddenly you have to learn how to live by the inner witness or inner impression from your spirit man bearing witness with the Holy Spirit.

Often times you will have to crowd out the noise of the world to find out what is going on in the inside. But remember, the only way to do that is to get quiet before God and listen.

> The Spirit itself beareth witness with our spirit, that we are the children of God.
> —Romans 8:16

It is the Holy Spirit within us who will bear witness with our spirit that those things which God is saying to us are of God. You must have that inward witness, an inward report.

When it comes to matters of the inward witness, I have learned quite a bit from Dad Hagin, who put it this way in his book, *How to be Led by the Spirit.*

> "God's Spirit bears witness with our spirit. Sometimes you cannot explain exactly how you know, but you just know it down on the inside of you. You have an inward witness that you are a child of God.
>
> You know that you are saved. You have a witness by the Spirit on the inside of you that agrees to that. And that is the number one way that God speaks to His children, by the inward witness."

Dad Hagin was speaking from Proverbs 20:27 . . .

> The spirit of man is the candle [lamp] of the
> LORD, searching all the inward parts of the belly.

He continues by telling us that,

> "God will enlighten us. He will guide us
> through our inner spirit. God said it is the spirit
> of man that is the candle of the Lord. All of
> God's children have the Spirit of God within
> them and can expect to be guided by Him. No
> one under the Old Covenant except the king, the
> priests and the prophet had the Holy Spirit
> resting upon them. But in the New Covenant, we
> have the Holy Spirit within us. The Holy Spirit
> bears witness with our spirit on the inside."

Everything that God does in our lives is through our
spirits. Think of the number of Christians that try to serve
God through their minds. They have not learned to tap
into their spirit.

One of the greatest lessons that you can learn is how to
be led by the Spirit, by the inward witness. It is not a lesson
taught in school. It has to be taught by the Holy Spirit.
Remember, it is the Holy Spirit that bears witness with our
spirit.

> For Thou will light my candle: the LORD my
> God will enlighten my darkness. For by Thee I
> have run through a troop; and by my God have I
> leaped over a wall. As for God, His way is per-
> fect: the Word of the LORD is tried: He is a
> buckler to all those that trust in Him.
> —PSALM 18:28–30

The Lord will light your candle by the Spirit. As long as there is darkness you cannot walk in the Spirit. The Scriptures tell us that where there is darkness people stumble and are offended. But when light comes they no longer stumble. (See John 11:9–10.) Therefore, when the Spirit enlightens you you'll no longer stumble.

> For as many as are led by the Spirit they are the sons of God.
> —ROMANS 8:14

> . . . it is your Father's good pleasure to give you the kingdom.
> —LUKE 12:32

Where there was once darkness before we were saved, now there is light by the Holy Spirit, and there is no room for stumbling. It is the Holy Spirit that will enlighten your path. You cannot do it for yourself. Only the Holy Spirit knows all things because He is the Light. Therefore, we should not stumble in anything. If we practice going before God and refuse to move until we know that we have heard from Him, we cannot go wrong.

Now take my word for it. The devil plays dirty games. He will use everything He can to try to interfere with you walking with God. Every tactic of fear he can muster up will be used against you. But remember, fear is nothing but darkness. God did not give us a spirit of fear; He gave us a spirit of love, of power and of sound mind to combat the spirit of fear. (See 2 Timothy 1:7.)

I have learned from Dad Hagin that when the Lord speaks, His words will bring a presence of peace. If you are sensing fear, watch out! Rebuke it, because it is not God. The peace of God will bring peace to your heart. If you do not have peace, do not move. If you are in doubt and you do not know which way to go, do not do anything. Do not go to the left or the right until you have the peace of God. Stop struggling and trying to get ahead. Listen to God and do what He says and He will put you over. For it is His will for us to prosper in everything. (See 3 John 2.)

This is not an overnight lesson. Listening to God in your spirit or inner witness takes time, practice and patience. But you have to start somewhere. You did not get into your mess overnight, and you cannot expect to learn this lesson overnight either. So start now and learn to live from the inside and be led by His peace.

> And let the peace of God rule [umpire] in your hearts, to the which ye also are called in one body; and be ye thankful. Let the Word of Christ dwell in you richly [in abundance] in all wisdom; teaching and admonishing one another in psalms and hymns and spiritual songs, singing with grace in your hearts to the Lord.
> —COLOSSIANS 3: 15–16, AMPLIFIED

If you really let the peace of God rule in your heart and let the Word of God dwell in you richly, you will have a song and a hymn in your heart unto the Lord. You will move away from walking in fear. Even when there is all sort of hell outside, inside you can have peace. When everyone else is confused and wondering what they are going to do, you will have the peace of God that passes all understanding working inside of you.

This is what makes us different from the world. The world bases everything upon what they see from the outside, but we no longer live by what is dictated on the outside, we live by what is dictated on the inside. The Holy Spirit bears witness with our spirit that we are the sons of God. Therefore, we should never base life on what it looks like. Satan will always try to paint a doom, gloom and despair picture on the outside. But if we live from the inside, then we will have peace inside, despite the picture on the outside.

Having this connection will carry you through any situation. It can mean the difference between life and death, especially during the times we live in with lay-offs, cutbacks, down-sizing, recession, etc. We must learn to listen to God. Then, no matter what goes on we can remain calm and walk in peace instead of fretting with the rest of the crowd.

So let the peace of God rule in your heart and His Word and presence will bring a spirit of peace to you.

HIS STILL SMALL VOICE

Most people are looking for the miraculous and they let the supernatural walk right by them. If you are one of those Christians that always has to see the miraculous, you will get lost with this particular form of listening. I make it a practice of never getting caught up in only looking for the big, grand and super-miraculous. If it happens, I give praises to God. But I always remember this is a daily walk. I do not have to have the super-miraculous in the natural when I am walking in the supernatural, because I know that is where God is.

Often in looking for the miraculous, we miss God. Look at Elijah in 1 Kings 19:10–13,

> He [Elijah] said, I have been very jealous for the
> LORD God of hosts: for the children of Israel have

forsaken Thy covenant, thrown down Thine altars, and slain Thy prophets with the sword: and I, even I only, am left; and they seek my life, to take it away. And He said, Go forth, and stand upon the mount before the LORD. And, behold, the LORD passed by, and a great and strong wind rent the mountains, and brake in pieces the rocks before the LORD: [If you had been looking for the miraculous you would have thought that was a mighty move of God] but the LORD was not in the wind; and after the wind an earthquake; [Wow that really sounds like God] but the LORD was not in the earthquake: And after the earthquake a fire [Don't get too excited just because the Word says God is a consuming fire]; but the LORD was not in the fire: [So if in all these things it still was not God, it had to be the devil trying to deceive Elijah because he had fear in his life. And you can do a lot to a man when there is fear in his life.] and after the fire a STILL SMALL VOICE. And it was so, when Elijah heard it, that he wrapped his face in his mantle, and went out, and stood in the entering in of the cave . . .

—EMPHASIS ADDED

Just as with Elijah, you cannot get caught up in the big or the grand and what appears to be the super-miraculous. It is a rhema Word that quickens faith. The word *rhema* means "spoken." This spoken word from God will quicken your faith.

" . . . faith cometh by hearing, and hearing by the Word of God."

—ROMANS 10:17

93

Your Conscience

> I say the truth in Christ, I lie not, my conscience
> also bearing me witness in the Holy Ghost.
> —Romans 9:1

When can you trust your conscience? Here are three keys. First, when you are following after the Truth with all of your heart, mind, soul and strength, your conscience is a safe guide. Second, when you are seeking after the Truth (not doing things undercover) and have a heart after God, your conscience is a safe guide. And last but not least, when you live to please God in all things, your conscience is a safe guide.

Your conscience is the voice of your human spirit. Have you ever known in your heart that you should not do something because of an inward, small voice that spoke to you? And when you did that particular thing in spite of the voice telling you not to, you got in trouble. We all have had this experience at one time or another. The reason this happens is that we were not practicing seeking the Truth. When you do not practice seeking the Truth, you do not pay attention to your conscience. You obey your flesh more so than your conscience. However, when you make the Truth (God), the number one thing in your life, and seek after it with all of your heart, you lean more towards obeying your conscience. We learned before that the Holy Spirit lives in our spirit and bears witness with our spirit. Therefore, if our conscience is the voice of our human spirit and the Holy Spirit bears witness with our spirit, the Holy Spirit enlightens our spirit as we seek after Truth. Then our conscience (by the Holy Spirit) will guide us along the right path. But remember, as Paul stated in Romans 9:1, you cannot lie and do wrong things and be led by the Spirit in your conscience.

The key to the conscience bearing witness by the Holy Spirit is pursuing the Truth. Once you make up in your mind that no matter what, you are going to follow the Truth, your conscience is a safe guide. Whatever you do, do it right. Be honest, walk in love and forgiveness. Be fair, be just and be upright. If you do these things, then just as God told Abraham, He will be a shield and a buckler to you and an enemy to your enemies. (See Genesis 15:1; Psalm 91:4.)

Make this confession with me: I am born of the Spirit of God. God's Spirit bears witness with my spirit that I am a child of God, and the Spirit of God leads me and He is leading me now.

This is one confession you need to make every day as often as you can each day.

A WORD OF PROPHECY

The Word of God is a sure word of prophecy through reading, meditating, teaching or preaching. (See Hebrews 1:2; 2 Peter 1:19.)

I want you to understand that you do not need another human being to hear from God for you. You need to learn how to hear from God for yourself. As long as Satan can keep you believing that you have to have someone else to hear for you, it handicaps you. Do not misunderstand, someone else can bear witness with what God is saying to you. But when it comes to deciding whether or not you have heard from God, you must remember, the Holy Spirit will bear witness with our spirit. When God tells you something, you do not have to tell everyone. Hide it in your heart. If it is of God, the Holy Spirit will bear witness to it. The Holy Spirit will always bear witness. Even when someone gives you a prophecy, if God has not already spoken that word to you, you need to put that prophecy somewhere on a shelf.

DREAMS AND VISIONS

According to Nelson's Illustrated Bible Dictionary, visions are "experiences similar to dreams through which supernatural insight or awareness is given by revelation." But the difference between a dream and a vision is that dreams occur only during sleep, while visions can happen while a person is awake (Daniel 10:7).

Often God will awaken you with a particular scripture or scriptural song in your heart. Sometimes it may not be an entire scripture or song, but only a certain part of a scripture or a stanza of a song. It may even be just one word or a phrase. A case in point is "the Sower soweth the Word" (Mark 4:14). For me, that one simple phrase was a word unto the Lord. God used that one portion of scripture to change the lives of several people in my ministry and around the world through teaching tapes. For weeks, God constantly poured things into my spirit regarding this particular topic. It became the basis for several weeks of teachings and writings for me. It lingers in my heart and the hearts of several of others, even to this day. Whenever we are looking for and expecting our blessings, we always remember to look to the word that the Sower (God) has sown into our hearts. The word sown is the foundation of all our hopes, desires and promises from God.

In the Bible, people who had visions were filled with a special consciousness of God. In the Old Testament, the most noteworthy examples of recipients of visions are Ezekiel and Daniel. Visions in the New Testament are most prominent in the Gospel of Luke, the Book of Acts and the Book of Revelation.

The purpose of visions is to give guidance and direction to God's servants and to foretell the future. Daniel's vision, for example, told of the coming of the Messiah. (See Daniel 8:1, 17.)

But every vision is not necessarily of God. You may have had a vision or even a dream about something you think you want, or something that you are believing God for, but it may not be of God. The way to test a dream or a vision is to see if they can be supported by the Word of God. If you cannot support it by the Word, leave it alone. No matter what it is, the Word should support it. God will never reveal or cause anything to happen to you that cannot be supported by the Word.

> I have also spoken by the prophets, and I
> have multiplied visions, and used similitudes, by
> the ministry of the prophets.
> —HOSEA 12:10

I'm not trying to judge your dreams or visions. That is not my place. The only Judges of those visions are the Word of God and the Holy Spirit bearing witness with your spirit. So hold on to your dreams and visions until you are clearly able to determine whether they are from God or not.

WHILE PRAYING IN THE SPIRIT

> Wherefore let him that speaketh in an
> unknown tongue pray that he may interpret. For
> if I pray in an unknown tongue, my spirit
> prayeth, but my understanding is unfruitful.
> —1 CORINTHIANS 14:13–14

I made reference to information I learned from Dad Hagin's book, *How to be Led by the Spirit.* It states that,

> "God is a Spirit, man is a spirit and God contacts us and communicates with us through our spirit. He leads us through our spirit. He does not contact us through our mind because the Holy Spirit does not dwell in our mind. Furthermore, God does not contact us through our bodies either. It should be comparatively easy for Spirit-filled believers to locate the human spirit. Those tongues come from your spirit down on the inside of you. When you pray in an unknown tongue, your mind has nothing to do with it. You speak the words out physically, but they do not come out of the physical senses. You yield your tongue to your own spirit and the Holy Spirit in you. When you pray in tongues the words come out of your inner most being, your belly, or your spirit."

I know that what Dad Hagin is saying is true. I have personally experienced this on numerous occasions. On one occasion, I had been praying in tongues at our former church location. While I was praying, information just began to well up inside of me. As I began walking back and forth speaking in tongues, it came up out of my spirit to call California about some property we were believing God to give to us. I had our director of finance telephone the company that owned the property because now was the time for the property to be given to us. What you do not know is that he had telephoned them just two weeks before, and they would not have anything to do with us. They said all kinds of rude things to him. But do you know the difference between the first and the second call? The Holy Spirit had investigated the situation and prepared the way. He was leading and directing me to call at this particular time, and He had already prepared their hearts.

Now of course when I told the director of finance to call the second time, he really did not want to do it because of his previous experience. In the natural he was fearful of making the call, but he did so out of obedience. Well, low and behold, when he made the phone call, the company gave us the property! That's right, they gave us more than 40 acres of land for the kingdom of God! They had an entirely different attitude about the property. Can you imagine what would have happened had we let fear rule the situation, or acted out what we thought in the natural? We would have missed our blessings!

In the natural, there was nothing that we could have done to change their minds. The only thing that we could do was to be obedient and allow the Holy Spirit to do what man could not begin to do. He can do wonders.

Several of your business deals, your successes and some of your most important decisions will come while you are praying in the Spirit. If you are looking to find the will of God for a situation, you will find it praying in tongues. When you learn how to tap into the greater One that lives on the inside of you, you will go farther than you ever dreamed possible. Praying in the Spirit is another way the Holy Spirit will enlighten your spirit to the ways of God.

It is very important that you develop your heavenly language or speaking in tongues. It is your personal prayer language, your private line to God.

You will be amazed at what your prayer language can do for you. Think of the Christians that do not know how to pray in tongues. They expect God to say something through their minds. And that is where the devil gets involved. Paul says, ". . . if I pray in an unknown tongue, my spirit prayeth . . ." (1 Cor. 14:14). Moreover, it is the Holy Spirit that bears witness with our spirit that we are the sons of God. (See Romans 8:14.)

So, really it is the Holy Spirit that is in our spirits. When we pray, it is the Holy Spirit that gives us the utterance. What we do when we pray in the Spirit is to lend our tongues or our vocal chords to the Holy Spirit.

When we pray in an unknown tongue, our minds (understanding) are unfruitful. (See 1 Corinthians 14:14.) It is our spirits that are praying. It is the Holy Spirit who knows all things, and who is bearing witness with our spirit, and speaking through us. This is a part of His enlightening our spirits. He is giving light to us where there is darkness. When we pray in tongues, the Holy Spirit joins ranks with us against our infirmities (Rom. 8:26). There are many things in life that we do not know, or cannot do, or cannot even begin to understand. The Holy Spirit, who knows all things, reveals them to us. When the Holy Spirit takes over to enlighten us, He uses our spirit-man to teach us that we might know the will of God. (See 1 Corinthians 2:12.) He is down on the inside of us to teach us all things.

Can you imagine how many Christians have cut God off and limited Him because they do not take time to develop their prayer language? Let me encourage you to spend time developing your prayer language and to spend at least an hour every day, praying in tongues and listening to the Spirit of God within you as you pray.

It is very important that you develop your prayer language and ask God to give you understanding or interpretation of what you are saying. If you pray in your heavenly language and you do not ask God for understanding or interpretation, you have not finished your prayers. As Paul states in 1 Corinthians 14:13–16,

Wherefore let him that speaketh in an unknown tongue pray that he may interpret. For if I pray in an unknown tongue, my spirit prayeth, but my understanding is unfruitful. What is it then? [since my understanding is unfruitful] I will pray with the spirit, and I will pray with the understanding also: I will sing with the spirit, and I will sing with the understanding also. Else when thou shalt bless the spirit, how shall he that occupieth the room of the unlearned say Amen at thy giving of thanks, seeing he understandeth not what thou sayest?

Simply stated, the same Holy Spirit that has given me the utterance is the same Holy Spirit that knows what is being said. And if I practice being led by the Spirit, not only will He give me the utterance but He will also give me the understanding.

But as it is written, Eye has not seen, nor ear heard, neither have entered into the heart of man, the things which God hath prepared for them that love Him. But God hath revealed them unto us by His Spirit: for the Spirit searcheth all things, yea, the deep things of God.
—1 Corinthians 2:9–10

Remember, the Holy Spirit bears witness to your spirit and reveals to you the things of God. The Spirit of God will investigate everything that is going on in your life . . . your business, your family, your home and anything that pertains to you, even the deep things of God. You have a Private Investigator dwelling on the inside of you and many of you do not even take advantage of it, simply because you have not taken the time to develop your prayer language.

The Holy Spirit will speak through you, after He has investigated the things that pertain to you. He will tell you what to do; what to say; and the way that you should go. He always sits high and looks low. He has already looked things over. He knows the outcome. And He will investigate for you.

Glory to God! Just knowing this makes me shout and want to run to seek the Holy Spirit while praying in tongues! What a privilege! He will investigate things for you and let you know which way to go, what to say and what to do! Hallelujah! We never have to fear or fret. For ". . . if God be for us, who can be against us?" (Rom. 8:31). Thank God we have an Investigator! Thank God we have the Holy Spirit! Glory to God!

I hope that you now see the importance of developing your prayer language and being mindful of the Holy Spirit that is on the inside of you. He is more than a man; He is God Himself, Who knows everything and all things. And just think, He wants to investigate things for you to show you what to do and how to make the right decisions. You do not have to lie, steal or connive to get ahead. Just be faithful and true to God, and He'll show you how to get ahead by the Holy Spirit enlightening you in your spirit.

God will not allow you to stumble as long as you walk in the Truth. He will enlighten your path. The only time you will stumble is when you walk in darkness. But He is the Light of the world. The whole world lives in darkness, but He has given you a light in the Holy Spirit. When you purpose to obey Him, you have your own Private Light. Again, you have a Private Investigator searching everything out that concerns you.

The Ministry of the Holy Spirit

One thing I want you to know about the Holy Spirit is that He is a Gentleman. He will not do anything you will not let Him do. You must want it and yearn for it. You must long for Him to come into your heart. Otherwise, He will not. He wants you to want Him. He wants you to invite Him into your life to lead you, guide you, teach you, instruct you and investigate things for you. But you must want the Truth, because He will only speak the Truth. He only speaks what He hears and what He sees. He speaks the Truth because God is the Truth.

> He that believeth on the Son of God hath the witness in himself: he that believeth not God hath made him a liar; because he believeth not the record that God gave of His Son.
> —1 John 5:10

If you are born again, the Witness is already in you. Your becoming a child of God is confirmed to you by God's Spirit bearing witness with your spirit that you have been born again.

Often after I pray in tongues and bathe a situation in prayer, I begin to speak things out in my understanding or even sing the answer out of my spirit. Remember, the same spirit that gives you the utterance will give you understanding if you ask Him.

In another passage in Dad Hagin's book, *How to be Led by the Spirit*, he states,

> "In Psalms 35:27 we are told to 'Let them shout for joy, and be glad, that favour my righteous cause: yea, let them say continually, Let the

LORD be magnified, which hath pleasure in the prosperity of His servant.' Let the Lord be magnified. He is not magnified in fear, but He is always magnified in faith. When you praise and worship God you are magnifying Him. You should always find time to magnify the Lord. Always find time to praise Him. The Lord told me that several years ago in a vision back in February 1959 that it is not just for my benefit but for yours too. He said 'if you will learn to follow that inward witness in all the areas of your life, I will make you rich. I will guide you in all the affairs of life, financial as well as spiritual.' I'm not opposed to my people being rich. But I am opposed to them being covetous. Some people think that God is only interested in their spiritual life and nothing else. But He is interested in everything we are interested in. The Lord has done for me exactly what He said He would do. He has made me rich. Am I a millionaire? No. That is not what the word rich means. Rich means a full supply. It means an abundant provision; more than enough; enough to give to someone else. I have got more than a full supply. I have got more than abundant provision. It is because I have learned to follow the leading of the Holy Spirit. And this guidance came to me by the inward witness. God will make you rich too. Only if you will learn to listen to the inward witness. Jesus said to me in that vision to "go teach My people how to be led of the inward witness."

Did you understand what you just read? Once you learn

how to follow the inward witness, to follow after truth and stay in faith in all of the areas of your life, God will make you rich. What does it mean to be rich? To have an abundant supply, to have more than enough! Remember, according to the passage I quoted from Dad's book, God told Dad Hagin that this was for ALL of the body of Christ, not just him. So you as a believer need to tap into this!

Let's make a confession together . . .

I believe and confess that the Spirit of God is leading me in all the affairs of life. He leads me in spiritual matters, financial matters and everything that concerns me. At all times, I listen to the inward witness, the Holy Spirit within me. The eyes of my understanding are being enlightened. I know on the inside what to do in every situation. God leads me by that wonderful inward witness, and I listen to it and obey it. Hallelujah! I'm not looking for answers, for God has placed them on the inside of me by His Spirit dwelling on the inside of me.

Confess this every day that you can, especially when it comes to making decisions. The more you confess it, the more you will allow it to get deep into your heart.

Over the years, God has given me many scriptures that have blessed me. However, when He first called me into ministry, He gave me one particular scripture that has continued to bless me, and I know that it will bless you. It is found in Psalm 32:8–9 . . .

I will instruct thee and teach thee in the way which thou shalt go: I will guide thee with Mine eye. Be ye not as the horse, or as the mule, which have no understanding: whose mouth must be held in with bit and bridle, lest they come near unto thee.

God told me that "living on the inside is one of the greatest things one can ever learn." He wants us to have understanding in all things. Therefore since He is the One that knows all things, what should we do? Turn to Him in every situation.

> For what man knoweth the things of a man, save the spirit of man which is in him? even so the things of God knoweth no man, but the Spirit of God. Now we have received, not the spirit of the world, but the Spirit which is of God; that we might know the things that are freely given to us of God.
> —1 CORINTHIANS 2:11–12

This is the purpose of receiving the Holy Spirit, that we may know the things that are freely given to us by God. He is the One that will enlighten our path. He will guide us, instruct us, teach us and show us the way to go. If we allow Him, He will lead us into all Truth, because He knows everything.

I trust now that you have a better understanding of the importance of being led by the inward witness. Remember that your head does not have anything to do with it. You must learn to be led from the inside.

> For as many as are led by the Spirit of God, they are the sons of God.
> —ROMANS 8:14

Seven Keys to Know When God is Not Speaking to You

Just as you need to know when the Lord is speaking to you, you also need to know how to discern when He is not speaking to you. Consider the following seven key things:

1. God's voice will never contradict the Word (Isaiah 8:20).
2. God's voice will never tell us to commit immorality (James 1:13).
3. God will build us up, but not flatter us. Do not look for someone to flatter you with a good word (Judges 6:12).
4. God's voice is not pushy or impetuous (driving). He will not force anything on you (Revelation 3:20).
5. God's voice will not inspire dead, religious works that are void of peace. Everything God speaks to you will create love and make peace. He is not the author of confusion. He always makes peace. If what you hear does not create love and make peace, it is not of God (James 3:13–18).
8. God's voice will not move you in a direction for which He has not been preparing you (Exodus 23:20).
7. God's voice will not cause you to become startled or confused (1 Corinthians 14:33).

Chapter Seven

Closing Thoughts

In closing, it is important to know that hearing from God takes time. You must desire to have communion and fellowship with Him. In the same way a husband, wife or good friend knows each other's voices because they have spent time talking and fellowshipping with one another, we will come to know the voice of God the same way.

It is His will that we know His voice. Four times in John 10, Jesus spoke to us about knowing His voice.

> But He that entereth in by the door is the Shepherd of the sheep. To Him the porter openeth; and THE SHEEP HEAR HIS VOICE: and HE CALLETH HIS OWN SHEEP BY NAME, AND LEADETH THEM OUT. And when He putteth forth His own sheep, He goeth before them, and the sheep follow Him: for THEY KNOW HIS VOICE. And a stranger will they not follow, but will flee from him: for they know not the voice of strangers.
> —JOHN 10:2–5, EMPHASIS ADDED

As the Father knoweth Me, even so know I

the Father: and I lay down My life for the sheep.
And other sheep I have [the Gentiles], which are
not of this fold: them also I must bring, and
THEY SHALL HEAR MY VOICE; and there
shall be one fold, and one Shepherd.
—JOHN 10:15–16, EMPHASIS ADDED

As lambs, we develop into mature sheep when we know
the voice of the Shepherd. Only as we develop in maturity
can God impart things to us that He desires to impart. So
we must purpose in our hearts to learn, know and develop
the inward witness. The only thing that will stop us from
receiving all the things God has for us is when we do not
obey His voice. We learn not to listen with our minds, but
instead learn how to listen with our hearts.

God wants all of us to be rich—spiritually, physically,
materially, mentally and in every good and godly way.
Above all things, He wants us to be in health and prosper
as our souls prosper. He has pleasure in the prosperity of
His servants. (See 3 John 2 and Psalm 35:27.) But you
must remember to guard your heart because out of it
flows the issues of life (Prov. 4:23). If your heart is not
right and your motives are not pure, you will not only
block the voice of God, but also the riches of God. Always
seek His face and His heart, and His hand will always be
there. He does not want things to separate you from Him.
He does not want things to have you instead of you having
them. So let nothing separate you from the love of God.
Let nothing keep you from pursuing Him, spending time
with Him and hungering and thirsting after Him.

When you keep your mind stayed on Him and your ears
always tuned to hear His voice, then you can say with boldness no weapon formed against me can prosper, and any
tongue that rises against me God shall condemn (Isa.

54:17a, author's paraphrase). No one will be able to take advantage of you. There may be those that think they do, and they may even cheat you. But in the end, as long as you stay in the Spirit, God will always return to you what you have lost. He said in His Word that whatever the enemy steals from you he will have to return it sevenfold. (See Proverbs 6:31.) Do not allow yourself to get in the flesh and try to strike back in some way. Believe the Word, follow after the Spirit, walk in love and watch for the manifestation.

Always remember, your prosperity will be based upon your ability to hear from God. It is what He gives to you—His ideas, His creativity and His way. It is not what we think of or want to do in our flesh that will bring forth the blessings. There is nothing in life that can happen to you that God will not bring you through and make provision for when you heed His voice. You may not see it, but provision has been provided for every situation. The sooner you learn this, the better off you will be.

God tells us to cast all of our cares upon Him because He cares for us. (See 1 Peter 5:7.) He will provide sweet water where there is bitter water, if you stay in His will. (See Exodus 15:23–26.) Do what He says to do. Go where He says to go. Do not move until you hear from Him and He will always be there for you. (See Hebrews 13:5.)

Moses put the tree of God in the water to make it sweet. There will be times that we will have to put God's tree in the water of our situation as well. You must know that in it is the Word, our Tree of Life. In every situation, put the Tree (the Word of God that makes all things sweet) in the water. No matter how bad it is or what anyone else is saying, the Word is our Tree of Life and it will sweeten any situation.

As God's chosen people, we need to follow His will by

hearing His voice; then and only then will we have peace. We must stop trying to be like others and follow God's will for every area of our lives, our marriages, our families, our churches, our businesses—every area! What may have worked for someone else, may not be God's will for you. In God's will there is peace. But there is no peace for the wicked. (See Isaiah 57:21.) A wicked person is someone who does not know God's will, or it is someone that knows the will of God and does not heed to it.

When you hearken to and have faith in the voice of the Lord, God's hand will come upon you and all that you put your hands to. You will make decisions with wisdom and knowledge that no man could ever teach you. Look at 1 Kings 18:44–46. Remember, Elijah prophesied about the rain and at the sign of it he sent word to Ahab to go to shelter so that the rain would not overtake him. Well, once the hand of the Lord came upon Elijah, he actually outran the horse that Ahab was on and beat Ahab to shelter! Now you know that Ahab being king had the best and fastest horse in the kingdom. But the hand of God upon Elijah gave him supernatural speed and endurance. It turned Elijah into another man! And God's hand upon us will do the same for us! God's hand upon you can supernaturally cause you to exceed your enemies' expectations and out do them in every situation!

If God has called you to a particular ministry, business or situation, you must know that the golden nuggets are there for you. But you will have to dig for them. Anything worth getting you will have to dig for to obtain. It is almost like a lost coin. It is not just going to fall into your lap. You have to get into the ground and dig for it. The same applies to what God would have you to do with your ministry, business or personal situation. You are going to have to seek Him, listen to Him and dig into the Word to have the success He desires you to have. Then and only then will you get the nuggets. The nuggets only come to those that are willing to pay the price to dig in and work for them.

Therefore, if God has placed it in your heart to do something in ministry, business or in any other situation, you need to pursue it with all of your heart. But remember, the first lesson you need to learn is how to listen to God. Without it, you may struggle all of your life trying to achieve success when His success is right at your doorstep.

Beloved, hearing from God will only take place for those that hunger and have a thirst for God and hearken to His voice. He will give you a word for every situation. Wait upon Him and He will renew your strength. Once you hear from Him, communicate to yourself what He is saying and write it down. Then, do what He says to do. Go where He leads and move as He moves. Hearkening to His voice is the key to your greatest blessings. Finally, always remember that the most important thing in prayer is not what you are saying to God, but what God is saying to you.

> *Confession: "We have the tongue of the learned because we hear from God. And we will not speak or move until we hear from the Holy Spirit."*

Commune with God. Talk with Him as your very best friend all day long. Put His company and presence first, above all things. Make it a practice not to go where He does not want to go and learn not to say things He does not appreciate. You must practice His presence all day, every day. Once you do, you will be astounded as to how quickly you will become attuned to His friendship.

It is very important that you make it a habit to talk to Him in tongues part of the time and expect to receive interpretation.

THINGS TO DO TO DEVELOP YOUR SPIRIT TO BECOME GOD-INSIDE MINDED AND TO HEAR HIS VOICE.

Immerse your spirit in the things of God
As you feed your spirit with the things of God, you become more sensitive to His guiding voice. As time passes, you can learn to let God guide you in the smallest details of your life. (See Romans 8:14.)

Read God's Word
Develop a love for God's Word and a consistent pattern of Scripture reading. Practice reading and listening to God as you read on a daily basis. Take time to be in places where God's Word is being preached with the anointing of the Holy Spirit. (See Proverbs 4:20 – 23.)

Commune with the Holy Spirit
As you pray and spend time alone with Him—an extended period of time on a daily basis—you become accustomed to His voice. You can sense it, know it and recognize it. You are aware of it.

If you do not spend time with Him, you will not be able to discern His voice when He speaks to you. You will think it is another voice or a familiar spirit. (See Psalm 4:3–4.)

Worship and Praise God
Spend time in places where prayer, praise and worship are centered on God. Prayer is a dialog not a monologue.

It is a two-way communication. Praise invites God's presence. God inhabits the praises of His people. (See Psalm 22:3.) Worshippers are the ones for whom He is seeking. (See John 4:23–24.)

Pray in the Spirit

I want to encourage you that as you pray more in Spirit, you will be in tune more with the Holy Spirit. Let me explain.

In 1 Corinthians 14:13–14, Paul said,

> "Wherefore let him that speaketh in an unknown tongue pray that he may interpret. For if I pray in an unknown tongue, MY SPIRIT PRAYETH [emphasis mine], but my understanding is unfruitful."

Spirit to Spirit praying is my spirit praying to God who is a Spirit with the help of the Holy Spirit. Then I ask the Holy Spirit to give me the interpretation or understanding of what has been said in the spirit.

Interpretation of tongues is also from the Holy Spirit. (See 1 Corinthians 12:10.) Paul said we could pray for our tongues to be interpreted. He adds, "I will pray with the Spirit, and I will pray with the understanding also: I will sing with Spirit, and I will sing with the understanding also" (1 Cor. 14:15).

You can alternate between praying in the Spirit and praying in English (or your native language). God will give you the interpretation to your own prayers, and you will become so sensitive to the Spirit that you hear God saying things to you as though someone picked up a telephone and called you.

Your Help Is From Within

Jesus said, "Howbeit when he, the Spirit of truth, is come, He will guide you into all truth: For He shall not speak of Himself; but whatsoever He shall hear, that shall He speak: And He will shew you things to come."

Let's take a look at some things Jesus said about the Holy Spirit. ". . . He will guide you into all truth . . ." He will lead you. He will guide you.

The scripture said, "For He shall not speak of Himself; but whatsoever He shall hear, that shall He speak . . ." The Holy Spirit does speak. Whatever He hears God say, whatever He hears Jesus say, He will speak to your spirit. Where is He to speak? He is in your spirit—and that is where He speaks. He does not speak out in the air somewhere. It is on the inside. He passes God's message into your spirit—either by an inward witness or by inward voice. Your spirit knows things that your head does not know because the Holy Spirit is in your spirit. Depend upon your spirit.

> But as it is written, Eye hath not seen, nor ear heard, neither have entered into the heart of man, the things which God hath prepared for them that love him.But God hath revealed them unto us by his Spirit: for the Spirit searcheth all things, yea, the deep things of God.
> —1 CORINTHIANS 2:9–10

You may notice that Paul said that God would reveal things to us by His Spirit.

Where is He living and abiding? In your head? No. In your body? In a sense, yes, but not exactly the way you think. The only reason your body becomes the temple of the Holy Spirit is because your body is the temple of your spirit. And He communicates with you through your spirit.

He does not communicate directly with your mind—He is not in your mind. He is in your spirit—He communicates with you through your spirit. Of course, your spirit does reach and influence your mentality. In Romans 8:27, Paul said, "And He that searcheth the heart knoweth what is the mind of the Spirit."

Practice daily listening to your spirit so you can have the mind of the Spirit. For the Spirit of man is the candle of the Lord. (See Proverbs 20:27.) The Lord enlightens us and guides us through our spirits.

God Speaks to us through:

1. *His Word*—Psalm 119:105, 130; 130:5–6; John 8:31–32; Proverbs 4:20–23
2. *His Spirit affirms directions*—John 16:13; 1 Corinthians 2:10; Romans 8:16
3. *Prayer*—John 10:4, 27; Jeremiah 33:3
4. *Peace/No peace*—Isaiah 57:21; 26:3; 2 Timothy 1:7
5. *Counsel of others*—Proverbs 11:14; 19:20

Are You Listening?

1. *God desires you to hear Him* —Psalm 81:8–13; 46:10; Isaiah 50:4
2. *You need to listen*—Psalm 4:3–4; Isaiah 50:4; Amos 3:7
3. *Prepare for listening*—Mark 6:31; 1 Timothy 4:7–8; John 7:17

4. *Your motivation for listening*
   - *Command*—Psalm 27:14
   - *Dissatisfaction*—Psalm 63:4–5
   - *Dark Times*—Psalm 63:6–7
   - *Lack of Understanding*—Psalm 73:16–17
   - *God's Love*—Psalm 143:8
   - *Need for Directions*—Psalm 143:8, 10
5. *Benefits of Listening to God*
   - *Strength*—Isaiah 40:31
   - *Directions*—Isaiah 30:21
   - *Refuge and Shield*—Psalm 119:114
   - *Closeness*—Psalm 63:7–8
   - *Instructions for Others*—Isaiah 50:4
   - *Courage*—Psalm 27:14
   - *Blessings*—Isaiah 30:18
   - *Satisfaction*—Psalm 63:5
   - *Wisdom*—Psalm 90:12
   - *Prosperity*—Joshua 1:8; Psalm 1:1–3

A Special Prayer
for the Reader
from
Dr. Hash

This is my prayer for you, my beloved brother or sister in Christ. I thank God for each of you.

I thank God that we all have ears to hear from Him and that His Word will not fall on dead ground but will produce and not return unto Him void. By faith, I know that the words of this book are the words given to me by the Father. By His Spirit, He will develop your ears to hear from Him. May the words of this book spark a desire, a longing and a craving in your hearts to know the things of God. I pray that the wisdom of God will be placed in you and that you will keep your eyes looking up to heaven, into the hills from whence cometh your help.

I pray that you will follow the leading of the Holy Spirit, who will reveal unto you the plans, purpose, and the pursuits for your life. In the name of the Lord Jesus Christ I pray. Amen.

In Appreciation . . .

My special thanks go to the following people:

To the staff and congregation of the greatest church, St. Peter's World Outreach Center of Winston-Salem, North Carolina. Thanks for your support and encouragement over the years as I have grown in the Lord and learned to be a pastor. I am glad that St. Peter's World Outreach Center is on my side.

To the editorial staff—Ron Jordan, Alexandria Smith and others who gave me encouragement and direction to pursue the publication of this book.

To our dear friends, Steve and Donna Houpe, for being faithful friends and supporting us through good times and bad.

To all who have prayed and given a word of encouragement and support—I sincerely appreciate your believing in me and letting me know of that belief.